D1118137

Dissecting Pinocchio

Dissecting Pinocchio

✦

How to Detect Deception in Business, Life, and Love

The Definitive Guide to Understanding a Liar's Body Language From Head to Toe

Christopher Dillingham, M.A.

iUniverse, Inc.
New York Lincoln Shanghai

Dissecting Pinocchio
How to Detect Deception in Business, Life, and Love

Copyright © 2008 by Christopher Dillingham

All rights reserved. No part of this book may be used or reproduced by any means, graphic, electronic, or mechanical, including photocopying, recording, taping or by any information storage retrieval system without the written permission of the publisher except in the case of brief quotations embodied in critical articles and reviews.

iUniverse books may be ordered through booksellers or by contacting:

iUniverse
2021 Pine Lake Road, Suite 100
Lincoln, NE 68512
www.iuniverse.com
1-800-Authors (1-800-288-4677)

Because of the dynamic nature of the Internet, any Web addresses or links contained in this book may have changed since publication and may no longer be valid.

The views expressed in this work are solely those of the author and do not necessarily reflect the views of the publisher, and the publisher hereby disclaims any responsibility for them.

ISBN: 978-0-595-48751-6 (pbk)
ISBN: 978-0-595-60831-7 (ebk)

Printed in the United States of America

For my grandfather, Freddie Gold Sr., a man who knew the ultimate currency in life is honesty.

"It's a basic truth of the human condition that everybody lies. The only variable is about what."

—Dr. Gregory House (*House*, Episode #121)

Contents

Acknowledgements

This book could not have been written without the assistance and support of the following people:

- Dr. Jeff Butler, *University of Central Florida.*

- Dr. Richard Pryor, *University of Central Florida.*

- Dr. Edgar Wycoff, *University of Central Florida.*

- Dr. Paul Ekman, *University of California* at San Francisco.

- Dr. Mark Frank, *Rutgers University.*

- Dr. Bella DePaulo, *University of California*, Santa Barbara.

- Dr. Stan Walters, AKA, "The Lie Guy," of www.kinesic.com

- Lieutenant John Bradley, City of De Land (FL) Police Department.

- Victoria Dillingham, my wife and confidant.

Introduction

Tell me lies,
Tell me sweet little lies

—Fleetwood Mac, *Little Lies*

I confess: I sometimes tell lies.

That's okay, because you do too.

Studies tell us that Americans tell between three and five lies per day, but this count depends on how narrowly one defines lying. For example, saying that you had a "great weekend" when you had a horrible one constitutes lying—but who really wants to listen to someone complaining about a bad weekend? And most assuredly, employers realize that potential employees will emphasize their strengths on résumés and during interviews while glossing over any weaknesses. One of the few times, after all, that we use our creative writing skills is when we are writing our résumés! If all our minor deviations from the truth were counted, I suspect the actual tally of the amount of lies we tell would be much higher. But doesn't it seem odd that so many lies are told each day in a society that claims to hate liars?

While most of the lies we tell are minor, our "blackest lies" are often reserved for those closest to us. Black deception—and how to protect you from it—is what this book is all about.

Philosophers have long struggled over defining when it is okay and when it is wrong to tell lies. Some philosophers have posited that it is *never* okay to lie, while others have attempted to place restrictions on using deception (e.g., it's okay to lie to protect another from harm, but it's not okay to lie for one's own benefit). In the end, all such attempts have resulted in failure. Lying is simply too complex an act to define by one holistic set of rules. What may constitute an acceptable reason to lie is one situation may be seen as reprehensible in another, although very similar situation.

LYING AND SOCIETY

Lying is certainly not always bad; in reality, it is often used as a social lubricant of sorts. We all tell lies in certain situations, like the false reason we give for leaving a boring party early or when we call in sick (when we really just need a day away from the stresses of the office). Lying is often easier than telling the truth and far less painful in many of these situations. Moreover, a well-rehearsed falsehood is sometimes more believable than the truth.

There are, of course, many reasons for lying. Here are a few situations to consider:

- Joe, who is an otherwise honest man, lies about his weekends to his coworkers. He comes in on Mondays, and when asked what he did on his time off, he talks about his kayaking and hiking trips. In truth, Joe stays home each weekend. He suffers from social anxiety, and his fear of parties and group activities keeps him from enjoying time with others. By lying about having hobbies, he doesn't have to attend uncomfortable gatherings.

- Bobby is 12 years old, and he accidentally broke his neighbor's window with a baseball. When asked about it by his parent's, Ralph lies and says another kid threw the ball. Bobby says he doesn't know the other kid's name or where he lives.

- Cindy is Kate's best friend. Cindy hates Don, Kate's boyfriend, and thinks Kate can do better. Cindy decides she can best help Kate by forcing her to break up with Don, so Cindy tells Kate that Don made a pass at Cindy.

As you can see, the above lies become progressively darker. Joe means no harm to anyone. He just wants to be left alone. Bobby wants to avoid punishment, so he invents an imaginary culprit. Cindy justifies her lying by believing she is "doing the right thing" for Kate, even though it hurts both Kate and Don. Successfully detecting lies requires us to understand a person's motivations to be deceptive. If you can figure out a person's motivations for lying—be it fear, greed, to protect others, etc.—then this will provide insight into how to avoid deceivers and/or get the truth from them.

If a person has little motivation to be dishonest, then he will usually be truthful. This is because lying usually involves some fear that the lie will be discovered and as a result, lying causes stress—and most of us are unlikely to invite more stress into our lives. This book will help you understand some of the reasons people tell lies and to use that understanding as a tool to uncover deception.

You probably think you are good, if not great at knowing when someone is attempting to deceive you. Studies show that most people believe they have a built-in "bullshit detector" that's been carefully honed through years of experience. Those same studies, though, as we'll begin to discuss, show that people are horrible at detecting deception. In particular, when it really counts—in other words, when it may cost you money, freedom or life itself—people are more likely than not to be deceived!

PEOPLE MISS MORE THAN 50% OF THE BIGGEST LIES TOLD TO THEM!

When I was a police detective, I interviewed victims, witnesses, and suspects every day in order to determine their honesty. I was sent to numerous government courses that taught me how to conduct interrogations, and later, I taught those same techniques to other officers as a State of Florida Criminal Justice instructor. I soon became widely sought after for my success in getting confessions from murderers, bank robbers, burglars, crooked cops, and other difficult-to-interrogate criminals.

I started publishing articles on interrogation techniques, created a research Web site (The Web of Deception) and eventually became an adjunct professor of Communication at the *University of Central Florida*.

My interest in lie detection continues to this day, and I correspond with researchers, psychologists, sociologists, and others in the scientific community who share my interest. In my studies and through my discussions with other scientists, I've found that people are generally very poor "lie detectors." Here's why:

- Research has shown that while people believe they are great at catching liars, in truth, they might as well flip a coin when trying to decide if someone is truthful or not.

- In other words, the average person has only a 50% chance or less of detecting deception—*even if warned beforehand that they may be deceived.*

- **Even more shocking:** Those people whose jobs **require** them to detect deception—including cops, lawyers, judges and psychiatrists—are not much better than anyone else at detecting deception. Actually, these people can often do worse than average, because their occupations make them more suspicious than the general public. They catch more liars (simply because they believe

everyone is lying), but are far more likely to believe an innocent person is lying when he is not!

- I've personally seen skillful liars manipulate otherwise intelligent people into giving up their life savings, get co-workers fired, get bigger raises than they deserve, and destroy relationships through lies and innuendos.

In this book, I'll refer to liars as Pinocchio. While conventional literary style dictates I should identify Pinocchio as a male, the real world demonstrates to us every day that liars comprise every sex, creed, religion, and color. Therefore, I use the male and female pronouns according to my whimsy.

WHY LIARS ARE SO SUCCESSFUL

There are many theories about why we are such bad lie-catchers. The most widely accepted reason is that we have a built-in "truthfulness-bias" that makes us less likely to believe others are lying to us. Think of it this way: if you had to examine every statement or fact presented to you, then you wouldn't have time to get anything done. Our truthfulness-bias, then, allows us to function in the everyday world unless something makes us suspicious. In contrast, think of paranoid schizophrenics: these are people whose illness makes them so innately suspicious of everything around them that they cannot function in everyday society. This is, of course, an extreme example, but an apt one nonetheless.

Another issue is that we aren't trained to recognize deception. Because we generally assume we are being told the truth in most circumstances, we fail to develop the subtle skills needed to recognize when someone is lying to us. Also contributing to the problem is that we have a lack of valid information about how people act when they practicing deception. Here are some examples that highlight this problem:

- A study using Secret Service agents, judges, psychiatrists, cops, attorneys, college students, and prison inmates showed the inmates were far more likely to detect deception if used upon them. This is believed to be because the inmates had more experience using deception upon each other during "high stakes" lying. Think of it this way: If you or me are caught lying about something, it's unlikely to be a life or death matter. For inmates, though, being deceived could and **often does** have life or death consequences. Researchers believe that it's this constant exposure to high stakes lying that gives prisoners an edge in lie detection.

- In another study, people were asked to evaluate a used car salesman's honesty and were warned that the salesman might try to lie to them. These people did no better at detecting when the salesman was lying than if they'd flipped a coin.

- Even though no weapons of mass destruction (WMD) were never found in Iraq and the failure to locate them has been widely reported by the major media networks, **over 35% of Americans somehow still believe we found WMD in Iraq.** The vast majority of these citizens cite "talk radio" or friends as sources when asked to explain their beliefs that WMD were found.

To further illustrate how our inability to consistently recognize when we are being deceived, let's look at a diagram portraying how most of us learn how to "detect" deception:

The Learning Cycle of Deception

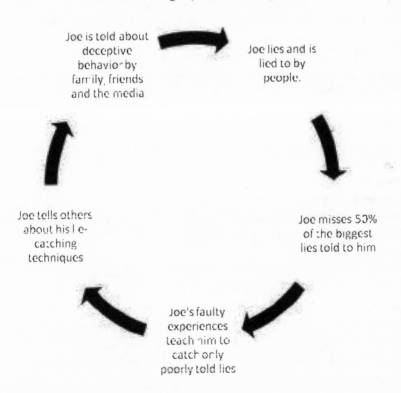

Joe is told about deceptive behavior by family, friends and the media

Joe lies and is lied to by people.

Joe tells others about his lie-catching techniques

Joe misses 50% of the biggest lies told to him

Joe's faulty experiences teach him to catch only poorly told lies

MISINFORMATION ON THE INTERNET AND TELEVISION

There is a lot of confusion and mythology surrounding the behavior of liars and how one can detect deception. Unfortunately, most of the information about liars and lying passed down to us by word-of-mouth and considered reliable has no basis in reality. Given that much of what we've been told about lying is false, it's only natural that this bad information is spread about on the Internet, where it multiplies astronomically.

An Internet search using the phrase "how to tell if someone is lying" will bring up 9,660 sites (as of March 12, 2007) giving advice on lie detection from alleged experts. The vast majority of these Web sites and "experts," though, regurgitate the same false and misleading information—sometimes repackaged and branded as "new" or "secret" information that has been "recently discovered."

The infamous Nazi Joseph Goebel once said, "A lie told a thousand times becomes the truth." In the Internet age, this has proven to be truer than Goebel ever would have dreamed. While we may not believe something we are told, we often give a lot of credibility to that which we read. Because of this mistaken belief in the written word, when we look for information on the Internet, we tend to regard what we find as being reliable and factual. Many Web sites that provide or sell information about lie detection appear on their surfaces to be knowledgeable and scientific. However, most have no scientific grounding at all, and while they may believe in the information they provide, that doesn't make it **valid** information.

Television, too, is responsible for a lot of misconceptions about the behaviors of liars. Unfortunately, television is a lot more persuasive than the written or spoken word alone and there is a great potential for misleading the public with bad information.

I was once asked to assist with the creation of a reality show that was going to "go inside" the interrogation room and show how cops spot liars. But when I pointed out that most cops are poor lie-catchers and that most interrogations are, well, pretty boring (until Pinocchio confesses), the show's consultants didn't care. They felt that they could "spice things up" by adding melodramatic music and narratives from actors who have played cops in the past, etc. I never heard from them again, and as far as I know, the show never got off the drawing board.

Whenever a character is being deceptive on a television show or in a movie, the show's director gives us lots of overt cues that let us know something is wrong. The ominous music and overly exaggerated body language underscore what's happening. **We** "know" what's going on, but somehow the person being deceives rarely does! Of course, the television and movie directors tend to use the same incorrect information about deception as everyone else, thereby reinforcing the same old, worn-out stereotypes. When I see these types of shows, it's almost like watching those poorly written horror movies in which the half-naked girl hits Freddy, Jason, Michael, or the Loc Ness Monster over the head once with an axe, throws down her weapon and then runs away. I feel like jumping up and yelling, "Hit him again! Don't stop until he's in pieces!!! *You are doing it wrong!!!!*

Sadly, most people out there are doing it wrong and providing misinformation to us on purpose. Why? Because it's easier to sell bad information then do the research into valid techniques for detecting deception. And if your methods don't work, well, you can just sell your next book (or advanced class) to the people who "need more practice."

The problem, as we can see, is that once we begin looking for the wrong cues, we tend to reinforce those mistaken beliefs over and over again. Only by breaking this cycle of misinformation and learning scientifically relevant cues to detecting deception can we avoid being deceived in our daily lives.

Let's look at from another aspect. We are products not just of our respective experiences and the various societal influences in our lives, but also how we interpret those experiences and influences.

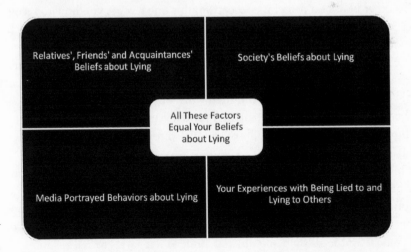

As you can see, it's very much a case of "garbage in—garbage out."

WHY THIS BOOK IS DIFFERENT

There **are** valid scientific data that can teach us how to effectively spot liars. Keep in mind that "effectively" means being able to detect 80% of the high stakes lies told to us, as a 100% consistent detection rate is generally considered to be an impossible feat.

This information isn't sexy or secret, and isn't known only by the CIA, police or government agents. Most of it is hidden away in scientific journals and papers that only other scientists read, although anybody could if they wanted.

Most of us would find these journals very boring and difficult to read; plus, the information on deception is normally scattered among many different journals. Although scientists are very interested in deception, there is only one journal solely devoted to deception research at this time, and it is only published online. Even more puzzling is that the research is sometimes contradictory; one study states A, another states B, and a third says C. One must look at all the studies, decide whether each one's methodology is valid and see which ones agree with one another. Often, one study sheds new light on an area of deception previously investigated by another study, and the two build upon each other. What we now know about human communication in general and deception in specific has dramatically increased over the last twenty years, and we learn more every year.

The purpose of this book is to serve as your guide to that research. But unlike other books on detecting deception, this one teaches you how to recognize deception body part by body part. It is, to my knowledge, the first and only book to map deception is such a way.

We'll start with exploring what motivates us to lie. We'll learn how liars use words and language differently than honest people. We'll then explore body language—starting with the head, and then work our way down through the rest of the body. Along the way, we'll discuss misconceptions about lies, liars, and lie catching. We'll end with tying all we've learned together and discuss some tried-and-true methods of getting liars to confess.

Think of it this way: if people tell several lies a day, and you (in your current state of knowledge) miss 50% of those lies, then you are at a distinct disadvantage in your personal, professional and financial relationships! Why be unhappy in romance, get stabbed in the back at work by "friends," or pay more for a car if you could avoid it all by being able, as Pink Floyd says, "to tell a smile from a veil?"

How much more power could you have over your life if you could cut through the web of deception surrounding you?

Some people, no doubt, would rather not know when they are being deceived. For those of you who are tired of being Pinocchio's pawns, though, let's start our examination with **why** our friends, family, lovers, co-workers and acquaintances lie to us.

I could have taken the easy way and written two or three books full of B.S. in the time that it's taken me to write this one (and probably made more money by doing so). This subject, though, is my obsession, and I have no interest in delivering anything other than the best information possible. I hope to impart some of this obsession to you.

Honesty is the most valuable currency we have in our society, and when you are sure others are being honest with you, you are truly getting your money's worth out of society.

For some people, though, ignorance is truly bliss. They won't want to know if their friends are lying to them, their spouses cheating, or their bosses giving their raises to someone who works less but plays the political game better.

Tragically, though, when that ignorance is transmitted to the whole of society, history teaches us that the price we pay is far from cheap. I won't press my political views on you, but it should be obvious to (almost) everyone that when we discover that Big Business, politicians, or religious leaders have abused our trust, there were usually warning signs beforehand, and I can teach you recognize those signs. Why should you be the victim of the next Enron, unfair taxation, or send your friends and family off to die in an ill-conceived war? Why, for that matter, should you even pay too much for a new car? If detecting deception can help you avoid those traps, then I'll be your guide to avoiding them.

Now, as the great Stephen King would say, let me take you by the hand and walk you through the dissection of not just Pinocchio's nose, but of his entire body.

1

Why Pinocchio Lies

I don't know why I feel the need to lie and cause you so much pain
—The Rollins Band, *Liar*

When I was a child, my dad told me it was wrong to lie and that "good boys never lie." Getting caught lying meant two things: punishment and the shame of disappointing my father. That isn't to say that I never lied as a child, but I always had my father's admonishment to remind me that it "wasn't right."

On an out-of-town trip to my grandmother's house, though, I learned that there were other rules to lying that weren't as clear-cut and easy to understand. On that trip, I was told not to tell my grandmother that we had visited my great-grandmother (her mother-in-law) because they did not get along. When I asked what I should say if I was asked if we had visited my great-grandmother, Dad pulled off the roadway and patiently explained that there were "white lies" and "black lies." He said that white lies are told to protect other people's feelings, and that black lies are told for selfish reasons.

When I asked more questions about when it is okay to lie, Dad became flustered and said that it's never "okay," but it sometimes "has to be done to keep people happy."

I have a friend who doesn't believe at all in lying. Years ago, he purchased a book that encouraged its readers to be brutally honest at all times—no matter what the consequences—and he sticks to that book's doctrine. I think that's a mistake …

My friend is not a popular man, despite being attractive and smart. His coworkers rarely ask his opinion on anything (they know they'll get a brutally honest opinion), but often describe him as "the most honest person" they know. Many people fear and loathe him because he doesn't "fit in" with society, **but if he would only lie every now and then, he would be much more popular!**

Over the years, I've come to realize my dad's explanation is probably the best that can be given about our attitudes toward lying. We realize that (most) people don't like lying or being lied to, but we also know that the world would be a much more complicated place if we do not tell the occasional "white" lie. Even though we profess to hate liars, we lie because telling the truth often causes more problems than lying. *As we mature, then, we come to realize that lies and lying provide societal advantages that the truth often cannot!*

People often prefer lies to the truth, and they can become quite upset if they're unexpectedly confronted with the cold, hard truth rather than a comforting lie.

Of course, the **reasons** why we lie are much more complicated than our **attitudes** about lying. There are many basic reasons why we lie, and those reasons can mix and blend with each other. (Scientists would say the reasons are not "mutually exclusive.") Let's take a look at some of those reasons:

• Pro-social: Lying to protect someone, to benefit or help others.

• Self-enhancement: Lying to make ourselves seem more important to others.

• Selfish: Lying to protect the self, conceal a misdeed, avoid embarrassment, disapproval or punishment.

• Anti-social: Lying to hurt someone else intentionally or to gain an unfair/unearned benefit.

PRO-SOCIAL LYING

Pro-social lying is probably the most frequently encountered form of deception we experience in our daily lives. These are the lies we tell when a girlfriend asks us if an outfit looks good on her or we express joy at receiving a disappointing gift during the holidays.

But these lies are also told in even more distressing circumstances. For example:

• What would you do if an abusive husband started pounding on your door, demanding to see his wife, and she was begging you to say she wasn't there? Most of us would lie to protect our friend—just as many Germans did during World War II when protecting Jewish friends from the Nazi regime.

- What if you knew a good friend had cheated on her husband, and the husband told you he had suspicions about his wife's behavior? Would it make a difference if you knew the affair was over? And whom would you be trying to protect? The wife, her husband, yourself, or all three?

Pro-social lying is generally considered to be harmless—unless you're hiding a criminal from the police, of course—and most of us engage in it. After all, when you ask a coworker how she is doing today, do you really want to know?

In reality, you and the coworker are engaged in a complicated social contract that allows the coworker to lie to you and you to accept that lie at face value. This is the "social lubrication" we discussed in our introduction.

SELF ENHANCEMENT LYING

Self enhancement lying is a common deception that many of us practice. These lies can range from "big fish" stories to those that make our social status seem much higher than it really is to others. There is some argument as to whether these lies are meant to be harmful or not, because raising your social profile can sometimes make other people feel less adequate in comparison.

Self enhancement lying involves many different behaviors and does not involve words alone. In our competitive society, social status can mean the difference in who is hired or promoted, gets a raise, attracts a desirable mate, and so on:

- It has been widely documented that taller men generally command higher salaries than their shorter coworkers. Because of this disparity, some men wear specially designed inserts or shoes that artificially increase their height.

- While men usually seek mates based upon attractiveness, women are more drawn by security. In order to increase their appearance of successfulness, many men will purchase expensive jewelry and cars. To accommodate those men who cannot or are unwilling to purchase the real thing, there are Internet sites that have thriving businesses in knock-off Rolexes and other high-dollar watches. Women, meanwhile, have access to breast-enhancement and collagen injections, along with other body-sculpting procedures.

- A trip to a nightclub will illustrate this principle. There you can see men advertising their success with social enhancing jewelry and clothing. Women tend to emphasize their attractiveness and fertility through revealing clothing, brightly colored lipstick, and carefully applied make-up.

- One television program made this point in an almost comical fashion: Its producers dressed an actor in shabby clothing and had him drive an even shabbier car to a restaurant. At that location, four women had been hired to evaluate men in terms of attractiveness and social status. After the actor received poor grades from the women, the producers dressed the actor in a suit and gave him a luxury convertible to drive back to the restaurant. Once there, not only did the four women fail to recognize the actor, they also rated him as being a highly desirable catch!

- On another segment, attractive and unattractive female actors pretended to be stranded on a roadside during rush hour traffic. The attractive females literally had men fighting to assist them, while the unattractive females sometimes waited a half an hour or more for minimal assistance!

It is understandable why we lie to increase our appearance of social stature. In many ways, our society bears the blame for these types of lies. Rarely does one see an unattractive person selling anything on television, and the implication of most commercials seems to that if we buy the right deodorant, drink the right beverage, and drive the right car that we can have anything (or anyone) we want.

SELFISH LYING

Selfish lying is another matter. This is when we begin to see the darker side of deception, and we've all probably seen enough examples to understand how it works. What is probably not understood as well, though, is that this behavior is primarily rooted in fear. As a fear reaction, it may not be based upon the circumstances at hand or entirely logical, either.

- During a murder investigation, I believed that a man, although he was not a suspect, was at the scene of the crime and may have witnessed it. After several hours, the man confessed to being at the crime scene and seeing part of the crime. His reason for lying to me? He had been meeting a girlfriend and was married. He didn't want his wife to know about his affair.

- If a person subjectively believes he is likely to be embarrassed or otherwise humiliated—even if there are no objective indications that such is the case—studies show he is much more likely to be deceptive.

- One prominent jury consultant, Dr. Jo-Ellan DeDimitrius, believes that people who are unhappy with their lives are much more likely to be dishonest than those people who are satisfied with their lives. This could be a form of unfocused revenge against those the selfish liar sees as better off, happier or of a higher social station.

Selfish lying is a form of self-protection; most people fear the consequences of their bad behavior, and lying may seem to be an attractive alternative to the truth. Here again, we examine motivations for lying: If Jeff is going to be fired if he admits to stealing, what can we do to make telling the truth more palatable to him?

Selfish lying may have deeper evolutionary roots than we imagine. For example, chimpanzees have very specific body language that indicates when they have found food; however, chimps have been observed in the wild to walk past food they have found and tightly control their body language. When they are certain no other chimps are around, they will then return to the food in order to keep it to themselves. However, other chimps have been known to keep out of sight and closely watch deceptive chimps to see if the deceptive chimps double-back to hidden food sources!

Nor is deceptive behavior solely limited to organic creatures. Scientists designed an experiment to test the learning and evolutionary abilities of robots. The robots were programmed to seek out food sources (electricity). However, one type of electricity was designed to fuel the robots while the other would "poison" them. If the robots found a good power source, they would glow green and attract other robots to the power source for communal feeding. If the robots found a bad power source, they were programmed to glow red and warn other robots away.

As the robots evolved through 50 generations or so, though, scientists observed some robots developed extremely deceptive and antisocial "DNA." Rather than adhere to their programmed displays of green for good and red for bad power sources, some of the robots would not glow green when they found a good power source and would stay dark. Even more amazing, those robots' descendents deliberately attempted to poison the other robots by glowing green when they found a bad power source! It appeared that in the competition for scarce resources, some robots developed a "selfish gene" that later evolved into outright antisocial behavior.

ANTISOCIAL LIES

Antisocial lies are the blackest we tell to one another. These are deliberate attempts to harm, undermine or sabotage another person's happiness for another's gratification.

Unfortunately, these are the lies most commonly told to us by those whom we trust the most, such as a relative, spouse or trusted supervisor. These lies are sometimes the hardest to detect because of

a.   The high level of trust inherent in these relationships;

b.   Our basic unwillingness to believe our trust has been violated.

We can all probably think of times when we've been told such lies and the emotional pain that comes with being deceived in such a hurtful manner. Antisocial lies are encountered on every level of social interaction, from abusive interpersonal relationships to corporate malfeasance (think Enron). Of course, these are also the lies told to us by confidence artists and swindlers, as well as by misleading or untruthful advertisers.

We sometimes blind ourselves to evidence that's literally before our own eyes, even though others often can and do see the deception (and sometimes in vain try to warn us). What is readily apparent to the outsider is frequently invisible to the person being deceived!

• If you ever want to see an example of this principle in action, watch some of the smuttier daytime talk shows when a man's fidelity is in question. The accused will sometimes be offered the opportunity to take a lie detector test, but before he does, the audience appears to already knows what his results will be. It's not that the audience is composed of people who are great at lie detection; it's just that the evidence is usually so overwhelming that a lie detector test isn't needed by anyone to know the truth other than the victim!

• Prosecutors often deal with outraged family members of defendants who insist that the defendant couldn't be guilty because "he's such a good man," even after getting multiple convictions for the same type of crime.In order to guard ourselves against any type of deception, we need to keep in mind the motivations of the person with whom we're communicating—does he have anything to gain by lying?

I once had a client who was upset with his insurance company because he felt his adjuster was lying to him about the cause of his $250,000 recreational vehicle's (RV's) breakdown. The adjuster claimed it was due to a manufacturer's defect—something not covered by his insurance policy—while the manufacturer stated the RV had been struck by lightning. The adjuster cited a particular component's issue he had discovered while inspecting the RV—a short circuit deep within the electrical system—**and** produced meteorological data showing there hadn't been lightning strikes in the client's area that month—while the manufacturer hadn't even inspected the RV. When I asked my client why he believed the RV's manufacturer over his adjuster, the client said because the manufacturer's salesman was his friend. When I asked how he knew this salesman was his friend, my client said, "Well, he's sold me three RVs. I don't know this adjuster from Adam."

When I suggested that the salesman had a vested interest in maintaining the client's belief that the manufacturer builds a reliable product (i.e., so the salesman could continue to sell the client RVs), the customer still insisted that the salesman was his friend and would never lie to him. Certainly, both the insurance company and the RV's manufacturer had motivations to lie in this case. But consider that this is just one claim among many for the insurance company versus the salesman who was possibly looking at selling the client his fourth $250,000 RV. The customer paid the additional expense of having an independent appraiser examine his RV, and when the appraiser stated he felt the RV's damages were the result of a faulty ground wire—just as the insurance adjuster had concluded—the client went back to the manufacturer, who grudgingly repaired the RV "as a customer service."

We are all guilty of following our hearts rather than our heads from time to time. Examples of this range from engaging in obviously doomed relationships to poor business decisions. We should try to evaluate circumstances more critically and less emotionally. Ask yourselves, "What would I say if someone else were in this situation?" You'll find even though you may not like the answer, it's better than realizing the truth too late.

In the next chapter, we'll start Pinocchio's dissection with the most troublesome organ of all: his tongue.

Things to Remember

- Not all lies are bad. Lying sometimes makes social situations easier to cope with than the truth.

- People usually have a motivating factor for lying. Ask yourself, "Does this person have a reason to be untruthful?"

- If trying to decide who is telling the truth in a dispute, what does the evidence tell you? And who has the greatest motivation to lie?

- Look at situations from an outsider's perspective. If you were an outsider looking in, what would you think of the situation? If an outsider wouldn't believe it, why should you?

- Past behavior is usually the best predictor of future behavior. If someone has consistently been dishonest with you in the past, then expect deception from him in the future.

2

Pinocchio's Tongue

*For millions of years mankind lived just like the animals until something
happened that unleashed the power of our imagination: We learned to talk*
—Pink Floyd, Keep Talking

With our ability to talk came the ability to lie. In fact, some social scientists have
proposed that one of the main reasons we developed the ability to talk was to
effectively deceive one another. And even though we are taught how to **talk** at
any early age, few of us ever really taught how to **listen** effectively.

Throughout the generations people have complained that "no one listens any-
more." We'd rather that children are "seen and not heard," and we groan whenever Grandpa insists on telling tales of the Great Depression.

We have become masters of tuning out that which does not interest us. We
are certainly overloaded with information everyday, and that makes it difficult to
pay attention to everything that is communicated to us. Even more problematic
is that most people are not effective speakers—they jump from topic to topic,
and sometimes seem to speak for the pure joy of hearing their own voices, march-
ing to the beat of their own internal drummers ... listening is hard work!

But in that process of tuning out, we may miss important cues to deception
that are sometimes very easily spotted.

<u>THE IMPORTANCE OF LISTENING</u>

When I was a detective, I specialized in interviewing suspects and getting confessions from them. It was rare that I did not get a confession from a guilty party,
and when I failed, I would go back over the subject's interview to review my performance. One interview in particular illustrates this tuning out process and how
we can miss important information:

19

"Tom" had confessed to breaking into a bunch of stores at night and stealing their safes. It took hours to get him to confess to committing these crimes, but the one thing he would **not** tell me is where he had dumped the safes. During the process of establishing rapport with Tom, we had discussed fishing—a hobby we both shared—and throughout the interview, he kept offering to take me fishing at his favorite lake. He even gave me directions to it and boasted about the fish he'd taken from it.

I, of course, was only interested in getting his full confession and recovering the physical evidence so I could go home. Hearing about this criminal's fish tales were not of the slightest interest to me. Despite what I thought was my best effort, I failed to get Tom to tell me where the safes were located. In my defense, it was late (2 a.m.) and Tom's interview had lasted all afternoon and evening.

After taking Tom to jail, I happened to drive near the road that lead to Tom's lake and it hit me: Was Tom trying to tell me where he'd dumped the safes?

A half an hour later and in water up to my waist, I discovered the first of all the safes. The next morning, divers located the rest: They were hidden right where Tom "said" they would be—in his favorite lake, and at his favorite spot in that lake. I just wasn't listening!

I often use Tom's interview as an example when teaching interrogation techniques to police officers, and almost every time, other officers tell me about similar experiences they've had. In most cases, the officers say how foolish they feel after realizing that the information they wanted so badly was being provided—had they only truly listened to **everything** that was said to them.

There is a school of thought that believes everything said in an interview is important and should be analyzed for hidden meanings. Of course, if you're not a police officer, it can get extremely tiring to pay attention to everything someone is telling you. But if you are suspicious of someone, then you should pay more attention to what is being said and how it is being said.

A friend of mine is a retail loss prevention officer who investigates thefts by employees and customers. One time, he caught a girl stealing jewelry. Another girl–who was not seen stealing anything—accompanied this girl. My friend arrested the thief and both girls accompanied him to his office.

But when he got them to his office, he could not find the jewelry. A female police office searched the girl who had been seen stealing the jewelry, but nothing was found. Just when the officer was getting ready to release the girls, my friend asked this girl where the jewelry was hidden.

The girl's reply was, "**I** don't have it!"

**Having taken one of my courses on interrogation, though, my friend real-
ized that the girl had told him exactly who did have the stolen jewelry!**

Somehow, despite the fact that both girls were under observation the entire
time, the girl who had stolen the jewelry had managed to hand it off to her
friend. I've personally viewed the videotapes myself, and I couldn't determine
when this was done because the two girls were so quick, but a search of the second girl showed that she had the jewelry hidden on her person.

These two thieves had realized that the thief was likely to get caught, and they
had perfected surreptitiously transferring stolen goods from one to the other.
They also knew that if you're not seen stealing, it's unlikely that you'll be
searched. What they didn't count on was their own use of language tripping
them up.

Had my friend not been listening to the subtle stress the first girl placed upon
one word in her denial, the two girls would have gone free.

IMPORTANT ASPECTS OF COMMUNICATION

Communication is a field of study that combines aspects of psychology, sociol-
ogy, and linguistics. Astonishingly, although mankind has been speaking for millions of years, we still don't know everything about it. We do know quite a bit,
though. For example, in a typical conversation, people only listen to 50% of what
is said, and generally recall only 25% of that 50% that they did listen to! Obviously, there is great room for improvement here.

Speech itself is composed of two main elements:

1.   Content. Literally, the words themselves.

2.   Meta-message. The emotions and relationship aspect of the message.

When we speak, we use more than just words to convey our thoughts and
meanings. For example, let's explore the simple phrase "I like you." How many
ways can you say it? Here are a few ways:

1.   I **like** you! (Meaning: Maybe more than you think!)

2.   **I** like you! (Meaning: Everyone else simply hates you, though!)

3.   I like **you**! (Meaning: I hate everyone else, though!)

4.   I like **you**? (Meaning: "As if!" or "Yeah, right! In your dreams!")

As one can tell, the emphasis we place upon our words can mean more than the words themselves. Communication scientists, in fact, believe that the words we use account for less than 25% of the meaning of our communication. This becomes especially important when dealing with Pinocchio.

ESTABLISHING BASELINE BEHAVIOR

Before you can judge whether or not someone is being deceptive, you first need to recognize his normal (baseline) behavior patterns. When looking for deception, we are seeking significant changes in the person's behavior in response to stimuli—usually a direct question—that is both timely and consistent. Here's what I mean by timely and consistent behavior:

1.   Timely refers to being anchored to the specific timeframe before, during and after the response. Just because someone's voice changes pitch or their verb tenses are incorrect doesn't necessarily mean he is being deceptive. My personal mechanic, for example, has an extremely hoarse voice that often sounds strained, especially as the day gets later and he gets weary. But that's his normal voice. However, if you believe some of the information on the Internet, you wouldn't trust him! Baseline changes are only valid if they occur in a timely fashion in response to specific stimulus. If someone's voice cracks all the time, then you cannot use that behavior as a reliable indicator of deception.

2.   Consistency is important because we want to focus on the area of speech that may be deceptive. As we'll discuss shortly, many lies contain elements of truth. The used car salesman may tell you wonderful things about a car's bodywork, brakes, and interior—and they might all be true—but does his baseline behavior alter **each time** he discusses the car's engine? If so, you may have a car that looks great and can stop on a dime, but its engine could be in need of serious work! The key here is that the change in behavior occurs when the person has to lie. He could be telling the truth 90% of the time during his dialogue, but it's when he's discussing that last 10% that the deviation from his baseline behavior will happen.

If you are a law enforcement officer or a corporate investigator who deals with the same people every day, I suggest you create a database that outlines the baseline behaviors of those you might have to interview. As a police detective, I created a large database that is still in use 11 years after I left the department. In that database, I detailed the verbal and nonverbal behaviors of everyone I had every interviewed. If I had to interview that person again, I would review the database beforehand in order to gain an edge in the interview. While I had many successes with this method, two interviews in particular stand out, and I often use them as examples when teaching interrogation techniques:

- Karla was Mindy's roommate and worked with Mindy at a local fast food restaurant. The restaurant's night manager noticed that a cash register that many people had access to was frequently short cash and the losses had exceeded several hundred dollars over a two week period. Since Karla and Mindy both used that register, I interviewed them and Mindy confessed to stealing all the money. Karla knew nothing of the thefts. But three months later, Karla was accused of stealing another roommate's jewelry. After reviewing my observations of Karla from the first interview, I stopped by her house. Karla's verbal and nonverbal behaviors were both markedly different from the first interview. She eventually confessed to stealing the jewelry and pawning it.

- Fred was an informant who had assisted me on many cases for money. One day, he claimed to have witnessed a store burglary; however, his behavior significantly differed from my other interviews with him. Fred eventually confessed that he had not witnessed the burglary and was implicating innocent people because he needed money for crack cocaine and the people he had named "had done other bad things." He was terminated from our confidential informant program and never used again. He was also charged with making a false police report. Had I not noticed the changes in his baseline behavior, at least two people would be in prison today due to his lies!

If you're not someone who interviews others for a living, you can still observe a person's normal baseline behavior. Remember that you're looking for deviations from the norm that are occurring as the person is speaking with you. If a timely and consistent deviation from the person's baseline behavior occurs when you discuss a certain subject (i.e., stimuli), then you need to ask yourself what is creating stress for that person.

DECEPTIVE COMMUNICATION

Liars speak differently than truthful people in many ways. Once you learn how Pinocchio speaks when he's practicing deception, you'll cue into these patterns quite easily. It just takes practice and a willingness to listen!

The first thing you must realize is that nearly all deception is planned ahead of time and rehearsed to some degree. Because of this prior planning, Pinocchio is somewhat limited in his tactics. He cannot predict every situation, response or question he'll encounter if his mendacity is challenged. Unlike the truth—which is usually easy to recall—deception requires lots of mental energy. Magnetic Resonance Images (MRI) of the brain show that lying causes the equivalent of an electrical storm in a liar's brain. This is due not only due to increased electrical activity, but also because of increased blood pressure and flow, in addition to the release of stress-related hormones like cortisol.

An even newer form of the MRI, called the Functional MRI (F-MRI), has shown that the brains of habitual liars are organized differently than most people: A habitual liar's brain has been shown to have **20% more white matter** in its frontal cortex than casual liars, and also increased blood flow capacity to its frontal lobes. While the brain's gray matter is used to solve problems and traditionally believed to be highly correlated with one's IQ, white matter is the "hardwired" portion of the brain and used for repetitive tasks. The brain's white matter gives you the ability to perform complex tasks without thinking about them (such as driving, knitting, or throwing a baseball). Either habitual liars have changed their brain's organization through constant use of deception or they are born predisposed to lying with greater ease than the typically organized human being.

To further explain the concept of white versus gray matter brain organization, let's examine a task most people can perform with relative ease and little use of the brain's computational power: Reciting of the English alphabet.

Most adults, even those with lower IQs, can readily recite "their ABCs" from A to Z without having to think about the task. This is because the brain has stored the A-Z sequence in the white matter portion of the brain. But if you were to ask that same person to recite the alphabet backwards (Z-A), an MRI during that task would show increased blood flow and electrical activity in the gray matter areas of the brain's frontal lobe (unless, of course, your test subject had memorized the alphabet backwards).

The same results occur when you ask someone to solve a mathematical equation or perform any other type of task that requires brain power. Habitual liars, sociopaths, and people with certain brain abnormalities, though, seem to have bypassed using the gray matter of their brains and do not show as much electrical activity when practicing deception. For the rest of us, however, being deceptive causes profound changes in brain activity. The physical stresses of lying (increased heartbeat, blood pressure, pulse and respiration, etc.) and its associated mental stresses—what one researcher calls the "trauma of deceit"—can also wreck havoc with Pinocchio's speech patterns.

Liars tend to exhibit the following speech patterns:

- **Higher pitched voices.** You may notice that when Pinocchio lies, his voice may rise and even break. This is most noticeable when Pinocchio is making denials about his guilt or otherwise protesting his innocence. Juveniles and females often are more susceptible to this flaw than others.

- **Speech hesitation.** If Pinocchio begins exhibiting more hesitation when explaining his actions, you might want to be wary. This sometimes means he is trying to "buy more time" in order to compose his thoughts. Note: Many people think that exhibiting speech disfluencies (i.e., stuttering, stammering, and other speech impediments) is a sign of deception. However, research shows that good liars are carefully focused upon their speech, and they actually make **fewer errors** than the truth-tellers!

- **Repeating questions asked of them.** If you ask an honest person if he stole Joe's wallet, he will normally answer with a direct "no." Pinocchio, however, often will say something like, "Did **I** steal Joe's wallet?" After repeating your question, he may then make a denial. Again, this is a time-buying technique. The dishonest person is trying to delay answering the question so he can think up a good answer and/or gauge your reaction to his denial.

- **Declaratory statements of their inherent honesty or good nature.** (Beware anyone who makes an assertion by saying something like, "I swear to God," or "I'm a Christian," or "I swear upon my mother's grave," etc.) Honest people do not need to bolster their credibility through reliance on outside sources. As a detective, I was trained to look for people who make these types of statements; an oath like "I swear to God" is of the best cues that someone is getting ready to lie. I've even had people bring in bibles or pictures of dead relatives to "swear upon," only to have them later confess to a crime.

Keep in mind that there is no one absolute sign of deception, and innocent people may exhibit one or more of these behaviors when excited, angry, embarrassed or otherwise under stress.

- What we are looking for are clusters of behavior that significantly differ from the way someone normally responds to questions.

- On top of that, we want to be able to focus on those behaviors and determine when they are occurring. If a husband starts stuttering and speaking more hesitantly than normal when his wife asks him about his night out with the boys, but wasn't exhibiting those behaviors before or after that topic, why does that subject stress him so much? Coupling indicators of deception to their specific stimuli is as important as recognizing those behaviors.

Up until now, we've explored some principles about Pinocchio's tongue that may seem very simple to you. That's about to change! That is because while changes in speech errors, hesitations and rate pitches are important, they are only **part** of our toolbox.

PINOCCHIO'S DILEMMA

A liar carefully monitors his voice and the words he uses. He does this because he knows that it is these facets of communication that can most easily betray him. He is also hyper-aware of his behavior and this can cause him to exhibit some characteristics that honest people usually do not.

As we discussed in Chapter One, most lies are preplanned and often are somewhat rehearsed. The daughter who has been out too late past her curfew may invent a flat tire that delayed her, and so on. But this rehearsal comes at a cost: Lies lack both the fluidity and elasticity of the truth in one's memory.

The truth, as my Dad was fond of saying, is easy to remember because it happened. But lying requires liars to not only remember their lies, but also to invent more details and fictitious events if their stories are questioned. Like a badly rehearsed play, lies frequently lack smoothness.

Lies, having been fabricated, are also subject to errors that can be found upon close examination. Of course, the more truth mixed in with the lie, the harder it is to detect a person's deception. In this segment, we'll examine not just Pinocchio's words, but how he uses them and puts them together in relation to the rest of his narrative.

This is Pinocchio's dilemma: He has to create a believable lie if he wants to succeed, but in doing so, he has to become a storyteller and must constantly mentally edit the story—creating more details as he spins his web of deception—which requires a lot of mental energy to create and then recall in detail.

NARRATIVE CONTENT ALLOCATION

Since it is hard to create details that never happened, liars tend to build around a framework of truth to support the lies. The problem, though, is that the lies generally lack as much detail as the truth, creating contrasts in the content. Consider this example:

- Detectives interviewed a man who claimed he came home and found his wife murdered. The detectives asked the man to write a statement telling what he did that day, up to and including discovering his wife's body. The man wrote several pages about going fishing that day, where he bought gas, ate lunch, and other small details. However, when it came to coming home and discovering his wife's body, the man devoted only one paragraph to this portion of the statement. He then devoted another page to detailing how he called the police and awaited their arrival. When the detectives focused upon the statement's portion that contained the least amount of detail, they started finding inconsistencies in the husband's story. The husband later confessed to coming home, getting into an argument with his wife, and killing her during the argument.

This is quite typical of the stories told by liars. They will allocate lots of detail to the framework supporting their lies, but the lies themselves are usually lacking in breadth and depth. Whenever you suspect you are being deceived, look for the areas that are addressed least by Pinocchio. You'll find this to be a very useful tool for detecting deception.

I recently analyzed a law enforcement interview for a client that involved the client's sister-in-law. The client believed her sister-in-law had killed the client's brother. After reviewing the video, I found that the sister-in-law's narrative was missing a chunk of time during an argument between herself and the deceased. But more even telling was the sister-in-law's improper pronoun use during one segment of the interview. Although the sister-in-law claimed the deceased had committed suicide, when discussing his death, at one point she said, "I can't believe **we** did it."

The detective who interviewed the sister-in-law, however, never caught that utterance. In fact, at the end of the interview and while the tape was still rolling, he called the crime scene investigators and told them, "This is clearly a suicide. I did a great interview and I'm satisfied there's nothing here."

Combined with the missing block of time and the pronoun change, my conclusion is that the sister-in-law played a significant part in the deceased's death.

Whether she killed him accidentally or assisted in his suicide, we'll never know. Had the detective noticed the improper narrative allocation and the improper use of the pronoun "we," that case might have turned out differently. (We'll discuss this case again later in this chapter.)

But let's discuss the proper use of pronouns first, shall we?

PROPER USE OF I, WE AND THEY

I can see you shuddering … relax, please! This isn't really a grammar lesson—not much of one, in any event. Changes in the one's use of "I, we, or they" are what concerns us here—specifically, any changes in their usage when Pinocchio is telling his story—not literacy itself. If someone is telling you about an event and suddenly switches from using "I" to using "we"—or the opposite—then that is an area that may need to be examined more closely. Let me explain a little more in depth about why this is important:

- By saying "we" rather than "I," many liars feel that less attention will be paid to their role in an event. It also adds some perceived credibility, because Pinocchio is implying that he has witnesses to his "good behavior." He also gets to dissociate himself from the others' bad behaviors.

- The use of the term "we" also implies a cooperative effort. If "we" did something together, than "I" don't shall **all** the blame because I didn't do "it" **alone**.

The term "we" can also imply an emotional closeness that is incongruent with the situation. I once investigated a rape involving a woman that made me immediately suspicious because she used the term "we" inappropriately. She claimed she had been abducted and raped, but every time she described the interaction between her and the "rapist," she said "we" rather than "I," "me," "him," or "he." In short, her pronoun use indicated more interpersonal contact than would be expected between a rapist and his victim.

For example, she described the rape as "we went into my bedroom," not "he forced me into the bedroom." At another point in her story, she said, "Afterward, we went to a party"—note the "**we went**" portion of the statement. Would you find it odd that a rape victim would willingly accompany her rapist to a party? I certainly did.

While this is certainly unusual behavior from a rape victim, in and of itself it could be contributed to shock and/or fear of embarrassment. After all, our legal system isn't known to be kind to rape victims, and many victims simply don't want to go through more anguish.

Remember, though, what I said about evaluating all evidence available to you and seeing if it adds up? When I researched this woman's history with my police department, I discovered that she had filed twelve prior rape accusations in three years! The chances of one woman being raped thirteen times in separate incidents within three years are astronomically high. I later obtained a confession from her that she made up the rape accusation because the "rapist" failed to call her after their first (and presumably last) date!

You need to pay close attention any time Pinocchio changes from using "I" to "we," because he could be trying to redirect the focus of your attention away from his actions. Likewise, if Pinocchio uses the cooperative form of "we" when it would be incongruous to do so, you should be on guard against the possibility of deception. Something else to watch, though, is the continuity and smoothness of Pinocchio's narrative.

<u>NARRATIVE CONTINUITY</u>

My Dad's saying that the truth is easy to remember because it actually happened is an apt one, and it exploits a weakness that many liars' stories lack: continuity.

One of my former supervisors, Lt. John Bradley, was a master at using this weakness to trip up criminals. He would very carefully and sympathetically listen to a suspect's alibi and ask questions throughout the story. Then, once he'd gotten all the "details" the suspect had to offer, he'd make the suspect tell his alibi again—but this time, backwards!

He'd also have the suspect tell his story starting from its middle and other points in time. The suspect would often get so flustered that he'd forget entire parts of his lie(s). John would usually get a confession—or enough lies to shoot down any false alibi—within a few minutes.

Lies often lack the smoothness and depth of the truth. The liar might pay a lot of attention to the parts of his story he believes will be examined most closely. But the parts that he does not give much attention to may seem like a bad movie; it may have missing parts or parts that don't seem to fit with the rest of the story. Consider these examples:

- One of the tell-tale signs of college plagiarism—stealing material from other people's works—and then "cutting and pasting" together a term paper—is that the segments often don't match one another. These papers lack the readability and "flow" of an original work. The complexity of the words used and grammar will often differ from paragraph to paragraph. There are companies that make software that compare the words students use in their term papers and calculate the probability that a paper is "stitched" together. These software packages will then search the Internet—the most likely source for the stolen material—and compare the paper to other written works on the Internet. Even if the words are changed, the software will still identify the original papers. This is because we are very consistent in the way we speak and write, which creates a "fingerprint" of sorts.

- Consider the JonBenet Ramsey murder case: The "ransom" note found at the Ramsey's home not only correctly spelled JonBenet Ramsey's name, but the note's composer also correctly hyphenated the word attaché using the proper French form (I needed <u>Microsoft Word's</u> help for that task). If the Ramsey killing was truly the work of a stranger, it was a stranger very well versed in the Ramsey family's life, as well as unusually literate and knew the exact amount of John Ramsey's bonus for that year (the ransom note demanded that exact amount). Most criminals are not highly literate, and when committing crimes of this nature, are not usually worried about spelling and punctuation! Also, JonBenet's killer used Patsy Ramsey's personal stationary to write the ransom note. Obviously, the Ramsey killing has many unanswered questions.

- In <u>Freakonomics,</u> authors Levitt and Dubner tell the story of their friend, identified as K. K. wanted to buy a house and was told by the Realtor showing it that because the housing market was "zooming," he was getting a great deal. When K. mentioned that he also had an existing home he was selling on his own without a Realtor, he was then told him that the housing market was "tanking," and too hard for people to sell homes on their own. Which was the truth?

Like a good tale, the truth usually flows smoothly from one part to the next. Even more importantly, those parts make sense when the story you are being told is viewed as a whole. Ask yourself, "Does everything add up?"

PAST TENSE VERSUS PRESENT TENSE

While we're discussing child murder cases, let's explore two cases that drew national attention: Those involving Pauline Zile and Susan Smith.

On November 14th 1994, Pauline Zile reported that her daughter, Christina Holt, had been kidnapped from a Fort Lauderdale flea market.

For five days, Pauline Zile appeared on national television and pleaded for her daughter's safe return. We would later learn that that poor seven year old Christina's body had been decomposing in a closet in her home the entire time, having been killed by her father for soiling herself. She was later found buried in a shallow grave in a vacant field (where her parents had hidden her after reporting her "kidnapping"). Three days later, Susan Smith reported her sons missing—the victims of an alleged car jacking incident.

Like the Ziles, Smith also admitted to having killed her children and putting on a show that captivated (and later, infuriated) the American public. What, though, did the public—and the media itself—miss in those initial interviews?

A study of these mothers' interviews shows that even at the early stages of their children's "disappearances," *Zile and Smith both referred to their children in the past tense—as if their children were already dead!*

Trauma counselors must often deal with the emotional aftermath of child abductions, and it has been consistently shown that the one thing parents of such crimes normally do is hold out faith that their children will return to them. It is exceedingly rare for parents of deceased children to begin to refer to their children in the past tense (as in, "he **was** a good boy"); rather, parents tend to speak of their children as still being alive ("he **is** a good boy").

In Leesburg, FL, Melinda Duckett, who killed herself after her two year old son disappeared, was found to have thrown away all his toys, a sonogram showing her son in her womb, and numerous photographs of him. Her son had disappeared on September 27th 2005. Melinda Duckett killed herself 11 days later (one day after her interview with CNN's Nancy Grace in which Grace implied Duckett was complicit in the son's disappearance).

At the time of my writing, Duckett is still the prime and only suspect in her son's disappearance. Having watched Duckett's TV appearances and listened to the CNN interview, I believe Duckett was being deceptive about her son's disappearance. The use of past tense verbs, vagueness of her recall concerning the events leading up to his disappearance, the emotional detachment exhibited by the disposal of her son's toys and virtual eradication of his presence in her apartment are all damning evidence. I believe Duckett's son is dead, and his mother was his killer.

We have great difficulty accepting the death of those we love, and it is hard for most of us to get rid of their belongings and those items that remind us of them. We even seem to extend this fixation on the present (or "living") tense to our pets. Last year, my wife and I made the difficult decision to "put down" our beloved 13 year old Doberman Pinscher, Brandon Von Dobie.

Brandon had been with us since he was a puppy. When he began losing control of his bowels and then his limbs, we knew what we had to do. It has been months since Brandon left us, and my wife still speaks of him as if he were alive. I imagine she will for some time to come.

People who commit acts of violence, though, who don't have those emotional attachments, are not fixated upon the "living tense." Zile and Smith are certainly prime examples of this rule, since they have proven their exception to it.

MINIMIZATION

When I had to put down my Doberman Pinscher, Brandon, I felt horrible. I knew that it had to be done, of course, but that didn't make the task any easier. We call the act of killing our pets when they are too old and sick to live a decent life many things like "putting to sleep" and "putting down" and, of course, "euthanasia." I fed him a piece of chocolate—a treat he loved—and held him as the veterinarian injected him with a lethal dose of tranquilizers.

What it was, though, is exactly what it felt like to me: murder. We just don't call it that, of course, because doing so makes dealing with the aftermath that much harder. So we soften the language and hope to minimize its impact upon us by using less distressing terms. While intellectually I know that I had to put Brandy down, I also know that if I told my wife that we "killed" Brandon that she'd be severely traumatized. So when we **do** talk about Brandon's "passing," we lessen our guilt by using less emotionally taxing words.

Liars, too, tend to minimize their acts and use softer, gentler words to describe their acts or the actions of others. In the previously mentioned example, something else the "rape victim" said raised my suspicions—or rather, it was something she **never** said: the word "rape." The next night after the party, this particular woman called some friends in tears and related what had supposedly happened to her. Her friends took her to a hospital and a doctor notified the police department about the "rape."

When I interviewed this woman, though, she never used the word rape; furthermore, when asked what should happen to the man, she said, "I don't want anyone to get into trouble." Most rape victims, in contrast, have no issue saying they were raped. And when asked what should happen to their rapists, they are quite vocal about their rapists being punished for their crimes.

Professional interviewers long ago noticed criminals rarely use words that portray them in a bad light (Hitler, remember, portrayed himself as a hero). Murderers will more often admit to "hurting" rather than killing someone, just as thieves would rather admit to "borrowing" rather than stealing!

Another cue that someone is being dishonest is to ask him what should happen to a person who has done something similar. One of my favorite techniques was to ask a suspect if the person who **really** committed the crime deserves a second chance. If the suspect said yes, then I knew that I was probably talking to the guilty party and not an innocent person!

It's amazing, but I've actually had murderers tell me that "the person who killed {him/her/them} should get a second chance." This type of behavior is called minimization. If you are asking someone about something you think he did, try to get the person to describe what he thinks "really happened" and "what should happen to the person who did this?" If you notice the presence of minimizing language, then you need to take a closer look at this person's story. Honest people usually have little or no incentive to use minimizing language when it comes to describing behaviors that have harmed other people mentally or physically. This doesn't mean that honest people won't use minimizing language, but they are far less likely to do so than dishonest people.

Even honest people, though, sometimes vary their language at times—especially when it comes to sparing other people's feelings. We call this language category "equivocation."

EQUIVOCATION

I once had a neighbor named Randy who was extremely handy. Every weekend, he had a new project to work upon. He once built a beautiful workshop by himself—he poured the concrete, framed the structure and raised the roof, etc.—in only two weeks.

Randy's house and yard were the envy of the neighborhood. One day, he invited my wife and me over to see his latest project: he'd tiled his kitchen and bathroom. When we walked into his house, we were both struck by, well, the ugliness of the tile! (Sorry, Randy!) When Randy asked if we liked the color scheme, we said the color scheme was "interesting." If we had been honest, we would have said that neither of us liked it, but Randy was a friend, and we certainly did not want to insult him.

The use of equivocation often comes when people are asked for their opinions and feel "forced" to give a certain response. It can happen during business meetings when discussing the latest budgetary constraints or over Grandma's Sunday dinner when asked if you want a second helping of a dish you truly don't like.

Equivocation is nothing more than giving a pleasant or ambivalent answer that hides your true opinion rather than telling the truth. What would you do in these situations?

1.   You see a friend's new baby for the first time, and in your opinion, the child is singularly unattractive. In fact, he is quite possibly the ugliest child you've ever seen. What would you say when you friend asks, "Isn't he **JUST** adorable?"

2.   Your boss asks your opinion of a new coworker. This person isn't learning the job quickly, but you know she has three children and is a single mother. If you give her a bad review, she may be fired.

3.   You're at a friend's party and not enjoying yourself. Your friend wanders by and asks if you're enjoying yourself. What will you say?

Equivocation is a true social lubricant. We realize that people often do not want to know the truth when they ask us our opinions. At other times, being entirely candid could adverse affect our relationships with our friends and family. In the delicate balance that society demands between honesty and deception, equivocation is the weight that keeps the scales from tipping to from one side to another.

I once heard a doctor tell a mother that her child was beautiful. She replied, "You probably tell **all** the mothers that." When the doctor denied that was the case, the mother asked him what he says when a baby is unattractive, the doctor replied, "I say, your baby looks just like you!"

QUALIFIERS

I'd like to tell you the truth about qualifiers, **but the thing is ...**

Qualifiers are words such as "but," "kind of," "like," "I guess," etc. We have all heard people say something similar to, "I like that idea, but ..." In other words, that person doesn't like that idea!

Some studies—including one that analyzed President Clinton's infamous Monica Lewinsky testimony—have shown that liars show a **400% increase** in the use of qualifiers.

If someone makes an apparently strong denial—"I did not sleep with her, but I understand why you think I did"—then that person is leaving himself a verbal escape hatch.

Other studies conducted into the use of the term "like" have shown that when people say, "I was there, like, at nine o'clock," they believe they haven't made a commitment to be truthful. They could have been at that location at six o'clock for all you know. If someone uses a qualifier in a statement, that statement should immediately be regarded as suspect. This is a person who either doesn't believe what he is saying or is being deliberately deceptive.

People certainly use qualifiers to soften their statements and to avoid hurting other people's feelings, but the end result remains that they are not making truthful statements when they use this technique.

EXPANDED CONTRACTIONS

People are generally lazy in their language usage, except when it comes to lying. Contractions—saying "I didn't" instead of "I did not"—are the normative use of language rather than the exception. Most of us—me included—tend to use contractions in our daily speech. And although we use contractions so frequently, when we lie, we seem to abandon them.

The most common and scientifically documented example of this phenomenon is when people are making false denials and state, "No, I did not" when asked if they committed an offense. John E. Reid—a nationally known trainer of law enforcement investigators—teaches cops to immediately be suspicious whenever someone says, "No I did not" rather than "No I didn't." Their analyses of thousands of interviews with criminal suspects show that this particular expanded contraction is a primary indicator of deception. Other studies have shown that liars show an over 100% increase in their use of expanded contractors!

USE OF "I DON'T RECALL" AND "I DON'T KNOW"

Let me unequivocally state that loss of memory due to physical and emotional trauma, as well as illness and exposure to drugs (including alcohol) is a very real thing. I have a high school friend who was attacked and left for dead in Los Angeles after a robbery. She is one of those people who is afflicted with true amnesia and it's a debilitating illness. That being said, permanent partial amnesia is an uncommon thing, and permanent total amnesia is even rarer.

Sometimes the easiest lie to tell is the one that has no details. This is often the strategy Pinocchio uses when he doesn't want to commit to a story that might not hold up to careful scrutiny.

What normally trips Pinocchio up is that, eventually, he has to have a starting point—something he recalls doing or seeing—before his memory conveniently failed, as well as a point where his memory became whole again. It's the marked difference in his memory's clarity between these events that should make you suspect he is being deceptive.

I've conducted many interviews in which Pinocchio recalled every meal he's eaten for a week, the television shows he's watched over the last few days and so on, but he conveniently "forgets" when he last saw his murdered girlfriend/knife/bloody glove, etc.

It almost gets comical when you compare what Pinocchio can remember versus what he cannot!

I once interviewed a man who must have watched way too many movies about amnesia patients; he pretended that he—for some unknown reason—lost all memory of his identity and had started a new life in another city. Unfortunately for him, his "old life" still had a nasty embezzlement warrant for his arrest. While he pretended not to know anything about his former life, he could tell us when his "new life" had begun. Unfortunately for him, a check of his "former" life's credit cards showed he had bought a motorcycle a few days after he suddenly regained awareness, and he used those same credit cards at various gas stations and restaurants across the United States before landing in his new city.

Next time, I believe he'll use cash!

In the case I mentioned earlier in which I was hired to investigate a man's death that had been ruled a suicide, the family was convinced that the man's wife had killed him, and that the police had ignored evidence that would have proved this was not a suicide.

Here is a summary of the case and its evidence:

- On Christmas Day, the man and his wife became involved in an argument. During the argument, the man threw a phone at the wife, which struck her in the forehead. He then grabbed a shotgun off a rack in their main hallway and ordered his wife to shoot him.

- When his wife refused to shoot him, the man placed the shotgun against the bottom of his chin and again told her to shoot him. She again refused, and at this point, the shotgun went off. The man fell to the floor and was obviously dead. The traumatized wife fled their residence to her father-in-law's residence and called 911.

- Officers arrived at the scene and secured it. The wife was brought to the station and was interviewed by the lead detective while crime scene investigators, along with the coroner's office, photographed the scene and collected evidence.

- The detective interviewed the wife for about an hour, determined she was being honest about the events, and released her after conferring with the crime scene investigators.

I obtained copies of all the crime scene photographs and the entire interview. Before watching the interview, I examined the crime scene and corner's report in order to get all the information possible. Here's what that information showed:

- In the kitchen, there was a broken portable phone on the floor. Its handset, battery case backing, and battery were lying in different areas. The kitchen was connected to the living room and the living room to a hallway. That hallway, in turn, lead to a bathroom on the right. Across from the bathroom door was the gun rack, which was mounted on the wall. Lying on the hallway floor was the deceased, with his head pointing toward the living room and his feet toward the final room—the master bedroom—which was further down the hallway.

- Lying between the man's legs was a single-shot shotgun. Its barrel was pointed toward his head and its stock toward the master bedroom. The man's left hand appeared to be blackened and covered with gunpowder residue. Looking at the crime scene, it appeared to be a suicide or accidental shooting death.

So far, so good, right? Then let's move onto the interview.

The detective began the interview appropriately by expressing sympathy for the wife's loss and obtaining her and the deceased's biographical and demographical information. Unfortunately, after that segment, things began to go wrong and got progressively worse as time went on.

When the detective asked about the events of the day leading to the man's death, the man's wife responded with, "He's been abusive to me before, but I've learned to get away from him when he got that way." (Did you notice the lack of the "living tense"?)

Given our societal reluctance to speak ill of the dead, this should have immediately set off alarms in the detective's mind. Whether it was due to improper training or an unwillingness to confront a purported grieving woman for political reasons, the detective didn't focus on that statement. Instead, the detective let the woman frame the interview—a classic error—and continued to allow her to dictate what they discussed throughout the interview process. Each time the detective asked a question, the woman answered with a "red herring" (an answer designed to lead the unwary away from the topic at hand). Soon, the woman painted a picture of an abusive, despondent man who hadn't worked in 20 years, who was incapable of sex during their 10 years together, and whose main activity was sleeping on the living room couch.

When the detective finally elicited a narrative from the woman, this is what he got (I'm summarizing here, of course):

1. The couple began arguing earlier in the day over a family matter. This argument was in the kitchen. The woman was standing in the center of the kitchen and the man was standing in the opening between the kitchen and the living room.

2. The man threw the portable phone at the kitchen floor. It bounced and struck the woman in the face. It then fell to the floor.

3. The man grabbed the shotgun from its rack in the hallway and shoved its butt into the woman's right shoulder. He then demanded that the woman shoot him. When the woman refused to do so, the man placed the shotgun's barrel underneath his chin. The woman, who was facing the man, backed away just as the shotgun discharged.

4. When her husband fell to the floor, she stated she ran out the door, got in her car and rushed to her in-law's residence a block away. Once there, she called the local police department and summoned them to the residence.

Here are a few of the problems with this narrative. First, the amount of information allotted to the events of the day was rather uneven. The wife gave a lot of information about the man's depressive episode earlier in the day, his simmering rage about the matter leading up to the argument and what he said to her prior to the phone being thrown. However, she said very little about what she said to him. And even more telling, there was a complete block of information missing: How did the argument suddenly shift locations from the kitchen to the hallway?

If you'll recall, the man's back was to the hallway when he threw the phone at the woman in the kitchen. But when he supposedly shot himself, the couple was in the hallway, but she is standing deep inside it while he is just inside its entrance. Somehow, the woman had moved past the man (who was standing in the kitchen blocking her way to the hallway). What happened? Did she suddenly run past him? Were there words exchanged? Pushing or shoving? Unfortunately, we don't know because the detective didn't catch onto this missing chunk of information!

What happened next, though, made it even more likely that the detective wasn't being told the complete truth about what occurred.

When the detective asked the woman some other questions about what occurred, she started sobbing and stated, "I can't believe **we** did it!" As we discussed before, the detective never picked up on that pronoun change and continued on with the interview. The detective ended the interview shortly afterward. The case was closed as a suicide and the body was cremated.

But had the detective done some additional investigating, he would have found a lot more to be curious about in regard to this loveless, sexless marriage. For example, a criminal history check would have revealed that this woman had previously been arrested for stabbing her husband.

Even more shocking to some people, when the crime scene investigators finished processing the crime scene and the deceased's body was removed, one of the deceased man's ears had been left behind. The woman, instead taking the body part to the morgue, threw the ear into her trashcan. Shortly thereafter, she disposed of most of the deceased's personal belongings. Incidentally, the body was cremated so quickly that the deceased's other relatives—who arrived the next day—never got to see it. This also prevented the subsequent investigators from measuring the length of the shotgun against the length of the man's arms and determining if he could even pull the trigger.

When I was brought into the case and asked to interview the woman, she declined to partake in any additional interviews. To this day, no one really knows what really happened in that hallway. I have my own suspicions, but that's all they will ever be.

PINOCCHIO ONLINE

As if the real world were not complicated enough, many of us these days now have entire alternate lives online, filled with people we have never met and will (likely) never meet. In some cases, we join virtual communities like the aptly named *Second Life* and even have virtual businesses, residences, and yes, even romances in these online worlds.

The same rules about Pinocchio's tongue apply to the written word in chat rooms, e-mails, and Instant Messages. In fact, sometimes it's easier to spot deception in the written word than it is when analyzing the spoken word; this is because with the written word, you often have more time to evaluate the content of the message.

While it should be a given that all is not always what it seems to be in the digital world, but unfortunately, people are forced to learn this lesson the hard way every day on the Internet. There are Nigerian 419 scams, "phishing e-mails" seeking your credit card and/or your bank account information, Web sites where stolen credit card numbers are traded for pennies on the dollar, pedophiles, and even serial killers operating on the Net. It would take more than one book to detail all the scams and dangers to the unwary; however, I can give you a few pointers on how to spot digital deception.

I have seen otherwise intelligent people fall for scams and be taken in by the most ludicrous stories that they would never have considered credible when offline. Unfortunately, much of the Internet—like a good science fiction or horror movie—requires some suspension of disbelief. In Second Life, for example, you can fly from destination to destination (something most of us wouldn't try at home). I theorize this suspension of disbelief, though, bleeds into all aspects of communication on the Internet, and by its nature, makes some people more likely to fall for the machinations of online predators. Combine that suspension of disbelief with our truthfulness bias, and it can be a recipe for disaster!

Obviously, those who are out to rip you off or otherwise harm you are going to be using sophisticated persuasion techniques designed to prey upon your greed or fear. The best way to avoid those people is to not answer e-mails from strangers (and of course, anyone purporting to be from your financial institution, law enforcement, etc.). The same thing goes for anyone who calls you on the telephone who requests personal or financial information. One of the many scams out there is someone who e-mails or calls you and pretends to be from your bank; this individual will state they need to verify your bank account number, Social Security Number, or other such confidential information in order to verify your identity and ensure your account has not been compromised. Surprisingly, people give out this information all the time. Think of it this way: Why would your bank, AOL, credit card company, or any other business with whom you do business need to "verify" your information? (They already have it!)

Research has revealed a few interesting things about how deception takes place in the digital world. Take the difference in the way men and women tell lies online:

- Men are more likely to lie about how much money they make, their heights, the vehicles they drive and other societal symbols of power. Men are also much more likely to be deceptive about the relationships they are already in (i.e., whether they are married or already dating).

- Women tend to lie about their age and weight, and tend to portray themselves as more open to relationship possibilities than men. For example, women may indicate on their profiles they are willing to date men who are shorter than them or of a different ethnicity, but in reality, they will not consider such a relationship in the real world.

There are also similarities in the way both sexes practice online deception, though:

- When using avatars—online representations of the person's face/hair/body-type—the less likely their avatar resembles their real body, the more likely both men and women are to be deceptive about other matters.

- Both men and women tend to be more honest in e-mails than they are in chat rooms, Instant Messages or during telephone conversations. It's thought the reason this is true is because there is less immediacy involved in e-mails and less threat of condemnation from the message's intended recipient. (I also note that it is becoming more fashionable these days to give performance reviews or terminate someone's employment by e-mail.)

- Other than the professional con-artists, both men and women tend to use evasion, equivocation, and vagueness rather than outright deception online. Just as in the real world, it is far easier to mix deception with the truth than it is to create an absolute falsehood. This again is because a blend of truth and lies is far easier to create and recall than a 100% falsehood.

- Surveys have shown that men and women find it more acceptable to indulge in deception online than they do in the real world. However, other studies have indicated that the more time one spends in the online world, the more likely both sexes are to be deceptive in the real world. Scientists theorize this occurs because practicing deception online lowers one's societal inhabitations against being deceptive overall.

The same rules about guarding yourself against deception in the real world apply to the online world and its communities, except that when you are online, you should realize that probably no one and nothing are what they seem or claim to be.

In the next chapter, we'll examine the part of body that most people claim they can use to spot lies: Pinocchio's eyes.

Things to Remember

- Active listening is the first skill you need to develop in order to determine if someone is lying. Unfortunately, most of us aren't good listeners and many of us aren't very well organized speakers. Because of these two aspects of communication, listening requires significant energy and concentration.

- Be on the lookout for higher pitched voices, more speech errors, and more hesitations than normal. These are signs of stress, and lying, of course, causes stress.

- Anyone who makes a declaratory assertion by swearing to God or insisting he's honest, a Christian, or "wouldn't do that sort of thing" is probably lying to you.

- Does everything you're being told make sense? Does it all add up?

- Is Pinocchio using minimizing language?

- If you're asking Pinocchio for his opinion, is he using equivocation rather than firm, concrete language?

- Is Pinocchio using a qualifier such as "but," "like," or "I guess?"

• Be instantly leery of someone who uses says, "No, I did not" rather than "No, I didn't" when asked if they did something.

• Pay attention to pronoun changes.

• "I don't recall" and "I don't know" are sentences Pinocchio uses to avoid commitment to a specific lie. He keeps his options open by using this tactic and limits your ability to attack his story.

• Liars tend to emotionally separate themselves from their victims after their wrongdoing. They may seat themselves further away in a company meeting, use less empathetic language or throw a spouse's ear into trashcans, but the end effect is an almost unintentional coldness.

3

Pinocchio's Eyes

You can't hide your lyin' eyes

—The Eagles, *Lyin' Eyes*

One of our most common misperceptions is that the dishonest tend not to "look people in the eyes" or engage in different gaze patterns than the honest.

It's not just lay-people who make these mistakes. Professionals whose job it is to detect deception on an almost daily basis also make these mistakes. One of the worst examples is the teaching of Neurolinguistic Programming (NLP) techniques to the law enforcement community.

THE HISTORY AND EFFECTS OF NLP

NLP was invented in the 1970s by a linguist (John Grinder) and a mathematician (Richard Bandler) who thought that by observing a person's eye movements, one could understand how that person was "hardwired." Once you understood how that person thought and related to the outside world, you could then better establish rapport with him.

NLP practitioners also believed that by observing where a person looked when asked to remember a past event, you could develop a baseline of his behavior. You then allegedly could later tell if he was really remembering or merely "thinking" (lying) when asked to recall an event. Sounds promising, doesn't it? There are, after all, links between the mind and body. For example, try this exercise: Sit in a chair and move your right foot in a clockwise circle. Now, with your right hand, try to draw a number six in the air. Most of you cannot, and those of you who can will most likely experience great difficulty in preventing your right foot from reversing directions!

Law enforcement officers thought NLP was a great tool and began teaching its techniques to FBI agents, detectives, and police officers in academies. Law enforcement officers were (and still are) taught that truthful people look in one direction when telling the truth, while liars look in another. I myself was taught this technique at two different law enforcement seminars.

Unfortunately, NLP has no basis in reality. There has never been any study that supports its claims—although there have been many, including my own, that show it doesn't work at all—but it is still taught to law enforcement officers across America.

Think of it this way: if you were falsely accused of a crime, would you want a police officer to assume you were lying because you happened to look up and to the left when asked about your alibi? No?

I've personally taken part in interrogations in which police officers have tried to pin a crime on an innocent person because they didn't like that person's eye movements. And it happens every day in interrogation rooms across the United States!

Why has NLP become part of law enforcement's toolbox if it has no validity?

Part of it is because police officers want scientific tools that will make their jobs easier. Another reason is that when a police officer attends a professional course, he assumes that the information he's being given is valid and that the instructor is an expert in the field.

However, a greater reason is due to our mistaken beliefs about deception and the eyes. We simply cannot get past our mistaken belief that liars won't look us in the eyes (direct gazing). NLP plays on this misconception by building on our biases regarding direct gazing and gaze modalities.

GAZE MODALITIES

Gaze modalities refer to where and how long a person gazes during interpersonal communication. In North America, we place great emphasis on "looking someone straight in the eye" when being truthful. People who do not look directly into other's eyes are often called "sneaky," shifty-eyed," and "untrustworthy."

The problem with this assumption is that it fails to account for two factors:

1. Different cultures have different standards and social mores regarding direct eye contact. For example, Asians regard direct eye contact with an authority figure or elder as being highly disrespectful. And even in America, there are

differences between Blacks and Caucasians when it comes to eye contact. For example, Whites tend to engage in more direct gazing when listening and less when talking to another person. But for Blacks, this pattern is reversed! This certainly has done nothing to improve race relations between two cultures that have shared the same continent for over two hundred years …

2. Since we were children, we've been told to "look someone in the eye" when telling the truth. What do you think is the first lesson an astute liar learns?

My own research and that of others has shown that liars tend to look you in the eye more often and longer than truthful people. This finding has been confirmed in numerous studies. There is no positive correlation between direct gazing and honesty.

You must realize, after all, that we have been told by our elders since we were children to look people in the eye when we are telling the truth. The direction in which one gazes has little or nothing to do with whether he is telling the truth. This does not mean that there are not liars who exhibit poor eye contact, but the good liars learned to look you in the eyes long ago.

I once had a burglary suspect who ate half the business cards on my desk. I watched as he ate business card after business card while I interviewed him, and after he consumed his 12th card—yes, I kept count—I asked him if he was hungry! But that doesn't mean all people would do the same thing; it was just a personal response to stress. The point I'm making is that just because you encounter one liar who acts in one way that doesn't mean that behavior is universal to all liars. The same applies to gaze patterns.

Sexual roles, dominant versus submissive personalities and various mental illnesses can also affect gaze patterns. Even drug and alcohol use can affect one's normative gaze patterns. One's gaze patterns also change from social setting to social setting. For example, if one dominant male gazes too directly at another dominant male for too long in a bar or at a traffic light, a confrontation will probably soon ensue. Social taboos indicate that one or both males break eye contact before a confrontation occurs.

In short, there appear to be far too many psychological elements warring with one another to consider eye movements a reliable indicator of deception. But there are still many so-called experts who claim eye movements can "reveal the truth."

It's too bad that they're looking in the wrong direction …

CAN PINOCCHIO'S EYES REVEAL HIS LIES?

There are ways in which the eyes can be used to identify whether or not someone is lying. For example, liars tend to show more dilated pupils and whites of their eyes than truth-tellers when accused of lying.

Notice that we are coupling two behaviors here: widening of the eyes and pupillary dilation. This principle will be stressed time and time again throughout this book: There is no one true sign of deception, so in order to increase our ability to spot deception, we look for multiple signs and manifestations of deceptive behavior. The more signs you can spot, the better your lie-catching skills will become.

Something else that must be considered is that in order for a behavior to be considered deceptive, it must be linked to a specific stimulus.

Let's take the case of Joe, who is suspected of stealing from his employer.

If Joe is wide eyed and showing the whites on all sides of his eyes the entire time we are talking to him, then this probably means that Joe is scared to death, but it does not automatically mean he's a liar.

This is a mistake that many police officers make when they question suspects. Many people are scared of authority figures, and their nervousness may often be mistaken for deception. But let's say we talk to Joe at length and develop a baseline of his normal behavior. We do this by discussing non-threatening subjects and then later, after we establish his normal behavior, we discuss the theft.

Throughout our talk, Joe shows no sign of deception until we ask if him if he has ever stolen from the company. This response is consistently elicited whenever we broach the subject of theft ...

If Joe exhibits dilated pupils and shows the whites of his eyes only when we ask if him if he has ever stolen from the company, then we have a behavior linked to a specific stimulus. Of course, we'll want more proof than just these two behaviors, but Joe's behavioral response to this question warrants further investigation.

Dilated pupils and widened eyes are primitive biological fear responses, allowing more light into the eyes and a frightened human to see better in the dark and more details, etc. Although we are not often hunted in the forest by predators, we are still hardwired to physically react to stress in the same primitive manner.

Now allow me to confuse you: although gaze modalities mean nothing in most situations, there is one situation in which a person's eye movements may be indicative of deception—and only one.

Let's say you are talking to someone and you ask a yes or no question that an innocent person should answer directly without hesitation. Here're some examples:

1. You think your spouse might have had sex with a friend of yours. You've been arguing about this person for some time. You ask, "I just want to know the truth. I won't be mad. Did you sleep with—————_?"

2. You think Jack has stolen money from the cash register at your business. You bring Jack in and explain why you're discussing the matter with him. After a few minutes you ask Jack, "Have you ever borrowed money from the company?"

3. The neighbors think your son Johnny broke their window. You tell Johnny, "If you did this by accident, just say so. I know you wouldn't do this on purpose."

An honest person may look away for a second, but that person will normally re-engage direct gazing with you very quickly. A liar, though, will often try to buy time while considering the "way out" you just offered. Liars will avert their gazes for a significant amount of time as they ponder this unexpected development.

Keep in mind, though, that this is no magical NLP trick and has nothing to do with how a person's brain is hard-wired. It's just a psychological ploy that sometimes throws the dishonest a curve ball. Honest people, though, have no need for excuses and will rarely take the bait you're offering. They even—as I can attest—tend to get very angry at the person offering the baited excuse. In later chapters, we'll discuss other tricks of the trade for eliciting confessions from Pinocchio.

INCREASED BLINK RATE AND EYE CLOSURE TIMES

Liars often show increased blink rates. These increases can be 20 times (or more) the person's normal blink rate, and can also manifest as a rapid fluttering of the eyelids. Interestingly, this sign of deception only shows when the person is trying to hide very specific information. This deception cue is very noticeable once one is trained to observe it, and is most useful when you are trying to narrow down your questions.

During an October 2005 interview on *The Daily Show with Jon Stewart*, former Senator John Edwards was asked several questions about his failed presidential campaign with Senator John Kerry. While Edwards seemed to answer most of the questions with ease, his response to one question in particular struck me as being blatantly deceptive.

Stewart asked Edwards, "How is John Kerry doing after the election?"

Edwards made the expected polite response and stating that Kerry was doing fine. But Edwards's face told another story: His blink rate increased dramatically while answering that question, and then decreased once the discussion moved on. But when Stewart broached the subject again later in the interview, Edwards's blink rate increased again, causing Edwards's eyelids to flutter uncontrollably.

Curiously, the only other time when Edwards exhibited this mannerism is when he was asked about his current relationship with Kerry; at that point, Edwards's blink rate increased again—although not as dramatically—when he stated that his and Kerry's families are now close friends. (My impression is that Edwards was "stretching the truth" when describing his family's closeness with Kerry's. In 2008, Kerry endorsed presidential candidate Barack Obama rather than his former running mate and "close friend" John Edwards.)

Another example of this behavior is the statements self-confessed child murderer Susan Smith made to the media when she reported her sons had been abducted in a car-jacking. As we previously discussed, Smith drowned her children and then spun a tale about a black male who forced her out of her car, taking her young children with him.

While Smith showed an increased blink rate when giving her interviews—so much so that I doubted **all** of her story from Day One—she also showed another sign of deception: increased eye closure time.

I realized that Smith's children were dead when she stated at one point that she knew "they were together and happy," and that she wanted them to know, "their Momma loves them." Smith's eyes stayed closed throughout her spiel, and although her acting wasn't very good, most people—including the media—bought it.

Had people watching Smith's face noticed her increased blink rate and eye closure times, I think her acting career would have been ended much sooner. As it was, Smith was able to tap into many people's racial prejudices (violent black man terrorizes young white mother and children) and wreak havoc in her community. More astute observers would have noticed something we'll discuss in the next chapter: the lack of agreement between her upper and lower face. As Dr. Ekman pointed out in one interview, "She's not a good actress, but she's trying."

In the next chapter, we'll examine the part of body that is so important to our social lives, there is a portion of our brains is devoted to recognizing it: Pinocchio's face.

Things to Remember

- Liars tend to look you in the eyes (engage in direct gazing) more so than truth-tellers.

- Looking up, down, left or right—or any combination thereof—means absolutely nothing in regard to whether Pinocchio is being truthful.

- If you ask a question that Pinocchio should be able to answer quickly, but he looks away and acts like he's trying to recall something, he's trying to come up with a story! This is called a time-buying mechanism.

- Liars will sometimes show dilated pupils and widened eyes as part of a fear reaction.

- Liars blink more than truth-tellers, but this increase is content-specific.

- Liars tend to close their eyes longer than truth-tellers; again, this is content specific.

4

Pinocchio's Face

I can tell by the way you hold your head,
Tell by the way you smile that you're tellin' me lies

—Krokus, *Our Love*

The face is so important to our social lives and development that there is actually an area of our brains devoted to recognizing faces. When a person is shown a human face this area "lights up" during a functional MRI scan. If this area is damaged, you wouldn't be able to recognize anyone's face—even your own!

It's no wonder, then, that when we try to determine if people are lying to us that we first look at their faces. In this chapter, we'll look at every facet of the face, starting first with Pinocchio's eyes and go on from there.

A brief word of caution when it comes to body language: Body language accounts for an estimated 80% or better of our communication. Therefore, when you are evaluating a person's words (what he **says**) versus his body language (what he **does**), you should rely more heavily upon his body language.

EMOTIONS AND THE FACE

While the eyes may be the windows to the soul, the face is their frame, and as such, every emotion the eyes portray must be support by the face as a whole.

What do I mean by this? By the time we reach adulthood, we have become skilled in putting on masks for the rest of the world. We rarely show the world our true selves, especially if we have something to lose by revealing what we are thinking or feeling. And liars usually have something to lose if their masks slip. A person may have "innocent eyes," but if the rest of the face screams "liar!" then those eyes are lying to you. Research has shown that there are over three thousand meaningful movements our facial muscles make to display emotions—we can make more, but they are usually the province of babies and are nonsense movements that we later abandoned as we age. Of course, some people have more expressive faces than others and can control more facial muscles than the rest of us.

This research also has shown that our emotional displays are universal: Fear, rage, and sorrow—as well as joy, mirth, and surprise—and easily recognized by all human cultures. This means that if a New Yorker is pissed off, an Aboriginal tribe member in New Guinea will recognize the rage on the New Yorker's face exactly for what it is!

But since we become so adept at concealing our emotions and putting on masks, this makes detecting lies through observing the face difficult to the uninitiated. Since we tend to scrutinize the face so much, liars take great pains to disguise any expressions that would reveal their mendacity. However, there are ways to unmask Pinocchio.

THE LOWER VERSUS THE UPPER FACE

While we can exercise tremendous control over our faces, we have greater control over some parts of our face than others.

We're taught from early childhood that it is impolite to express what we really feel when those feelings are at odds with the social setting. I can recall many a Christmas when one relative in particular gave me gifts that were less than thrilling to me. I knew, though, that my parents (as well as the gift-giver) expected nothing less than excitement from me. So I "put on my happy face" and pretended each Christmas that all the gifts I received were the greatest yet.

I doubt I fooled anyone—at first, anyway—but society often only demands that we make a good show at portraying the appropriate emotional displays, not that we be successful at the portrayal. Think of it this way: we go to parties we don't like and act like we love to be there; we attend the funerals of people we hate and act sad, and we pretend to be happy when other people receive promotions that we secretly believe we instead deserve.

By the time we reach our teenage years, most of us realize we are required to "put on masks" to disguise our true emotions in certain social situations; if we did not, we would cause ourselves—and those around us—more stress than if our true feelings are known.

Tournament poker players use many devices to hide their true emotions, including sunglasses and hats. These poker players are often experts in recognizing stress in others (and perhaps just as importantly, when another player **isn't** stressed).

Notice that when these professionals are looking to hide their emotions, though, they try to disguise or hide their **upper** faces. This is because poker players know that although we can exhibit amazing control over our lower faces, we have very limited ability to control our upper faces. Sure, we can smile and bluff our way through a boring company meeting and act as if we're excited about the latest advertising campaign; but if you look closely, do those smiles really "touch the eyes" of the person pretending to be happy? (Keep this in mind if you are plying poker and think you are correctly reading your opponent's emotions: In most cases, the emotion being portrayed is the opposite of what she's feeling.)

Whenever someone pretends to feel one way but actually feels another, there is usually a conflict between the upper facial expression, and the lower. In such cases, you should trust the upper face to accurately portray what the person is **really** feeling. The most often faked expression is the smile, and in particular, smiles of enjoyment. If a smile terminates below the eyes—true smiles of enjoyment involve the outer and upper muscles of the eyes, causing them to crinkle and lift the outer corners of the eyes upward—then it is a false smile.

This also applies to expressions of grief. Many times, deceptive people will express sadness or remorse when they don't feel it in an attempt to manipulate you. Tears may flow and the person may be choked up, but if the person's expression of grief is confined to her lower face, watch out! This lack of grief was very evident in Susan Smith's upper face when she pretended to be in shock at her children's "kidnappings." Although she played the part of a distressed mother, the upper portion of her face never agreed with its lower counterpart.

All emotions have effects on both the upper and lower parts of the face. It takes just a little practice to recognize the difference between false emotional and true displays (for further information on this topic, I highly recommend you read Dr. Ekman's book, *Unmasking the Face*, which has excellent pictures). Take a bride at her wedding: she may be smiling, but she may also be simultaneously weeping. In this case, you must look the overall face and recognize that sadness involves more than just crying. Are the bride's inner eyelids contorted upward in the typical grief expression? Does her forehead have wrinkled vertical lines between the eyes?

If the answer to those questions is "no," then she is crying out of joy, not sadness. But if those signs of grief are present, then something is seriously wrong. Just as crying at a wedding may be a sign of happiness rather than sadness, smiles at a funeral do not (necessarily) mean one is happy. The true emotion(s) will always be seen in the upper part of the face.

THE ONE SECOND FRIENDSHIP TEST

Have you ever wondered if someone truly likes you or if they are merely pretend-ing to do so? I get great pleasure out of watching people when I accompany my wife to the local malls in our city. Since I am not someone who enjoys shopping, I amuse myself by watching the interactions that occur between people. I've found that I can accurately predict which people are friends just by watching their upper faces when they approach one another.

While strangers and friends alike may smile when approaching one another, watch their upper faces—in particular, their eyes and eyebrows. People who truly like each another almost invariably greet each other by smiling genuine smiles (ones that touch the eyes) accompanied by a **quick raising of the eyebrows**. If you ever want to know if someone truly likes you, quickly raise your eyebrows when greeting that person. If you do not receive a similar response, you are being deceived; that person is not your friend!

I've often used this technique in the workplace to determine who is my friend or foe, and the technique has withstood the test of time. I've had subordinates, coworkers, and supervisors who all outwardly appeared to be friendly to me, but in each case, those who would not raise their eyebrows in return to my greeting (or initiate it themselves) have all turned out to be back-stabbing pretenders.

Again, we are relying upon the upper face to judge how a person truly feels in this case. Smiling can be done by nearly anyone, but emotions that are truly felt are always reflected in the upper part of the face. Granted, in this case, this is an expression that can be faked, but rarely is for some reason.

SYMMETRY OF FACIAL EXPRESSIONS

True emotional displays—as opposed to the false or social masks we often have to wear—are symmetrical. In other words, they are equal to both sides of the face. When one is trying to convey an emotion, however, the result is usually displayed unequally. There is probably no better example of this phenomenon than George W. Bush, the 43rd President of the United States.

When George W. Bush genuinely smiles, his smiles are symmetrical; however, he has often been criticized because he appears to sneer during speeches and public appearances. Those sneers are actually poorly executed and asymmetrical social smiles.

Most people fail to recognize asymmetrical facial expressions as false expressions. These are truly masks that are intended to fool you into believing the person is feeling one thing when they feel something quite different. Nor are these expressions limited to smiles. People may grimace to show distaste, but if the grimace isn't equal from side-to-side, the person may be affecting distaste because she thinks it's what she's supposed to do, not what she feels! Think of it like laughter: We may laugh at jokes that we don't think are funny, but we laugh because those around us are laughing.

Look around you next time you're in one of those social situations and see how many of those smiling and laughing are really wearing masks. If the smiles don't touch the eyes and are asymmetrical, then these are social expressions. And if you are in a mixed crowd and see a lot of these social expressions when someone tells an off-color joke, beware of responding with a joke of your own! One of the most tired expressions I've heard while conducting Internal Affairs investigations into complaints was, "But she laughed at the joke too!"

TIMING OF EMOTIONAL DISPLAYS AND FLUIDITY OF EMOTIONS

Timing is another often-overlooked facet of interpersonal communication. When we talk to one another, there is a negotiated ebb-and-flow to the conversation. We tend to negotiate who speaks and for how long before interrupting one another with questions and comments.

Facial expressions, though, are not negotiated in the same manner. While you may wait patiently to speak your turn, your facial expressions that reflect your true emotions will not.

I once interviewed a man who was accused of embezzling from his company. Before going into the interview, I was warned that the man had a violent temper and was highly upset at being accused of being a thief. One thing I always ask in my interviews is, "How do you feel about being a suspect?"

The man began pounding his fists upon the table and said he was angry, and his face began contorting in rage. I let him go on for a few minutes, and then I started laughing. The man looked at me as if I were insane, then he went back to punctuating his expression of anger by pounding on the table.

When he'd finished, I told him that I knew he was not telling me everything he knew about the theft, and that if he was done exercising, we needed to talk. An hour later, he confessed to taking thousands of dollars of equipment and money from his employer. What do you think cued me into the fact that he was putting on a show?

Here is a simple concept I'd like you to remember, whether you're discussing infidelity with your spouse or conducting a homicide investigation: facial expressions of true emotions always come before words or physical actions. Always!

If you accuse your husband of cheating and he gets a hurt expression on his face, then he says his feelings are hurt, he may be innocent of the accusation. But if he says his feelings are hurt and **then** puts on an emotional display, he's faking his emotional pain!

Remember that we have only limited control over our upper face. It's where true emotions can be correctly interpreted as being real. We've all been with people who have become upset at bad news, been startled or lost their tempers.

The first thing that happens when someone receives bad news is their faces crumble in sadness; if they become scared, their eyes widen in fear; if angered, their foreheads and brows knit together in a fierce look. **Then** they may pound tables, but not before! (This same scenario was played out in the 1997 film, *The Rainmaker*, when the lawyer played by Matt Damon feigns anger during a courtroom scene. Damon, an exceptional actor, pounds a table **before** his face fully registers his fake anger. Whether or not this was an intentional omission by Damon, it is an exceptional example of this principle.)

The embezzler we just discussed had learned that he could intimidate people by pretending to have a bad temper and bullying others, but he never learned the secret of timing his emotional displays. After I arrested him—keeping in mind that I'm 5'09 tall and weigh 160 pounds, while he was 6'03 tall and weighed 210 pounds—this "frightening" guy who'd terrorized his coworkers cried more than most women that I'd ever arrested. He later told me that he'd never been in a fight because he'd always been able to scare off other men by making fearsome faces when threatened. When we walked out to my car, he was trembling so hard I thought he might have a heart attack.

There was another aspect to that particular interview, though, that is very important to remember: the extreme fluidity of the man's emotions. When we get upset, we normally do not "switch" on and off those reactions at will. But when I laughed at our posturing thief, he forgot to "act angry" for a moment because what he was really feeling was puzzlement.

Whenever you find that a person is rapidly switching from one emotional state or expression to another, this is generally a sign of deception. In such cases, the person is literally trying to find the right emotion that'll work on you, much like a burglar trying random keys on a lock hoping to find one that fits. Children are notorious for using this tactic upon their parents: they'll cry, beg, shout and threaten to accomplish their goals. In adults, I've found that women are more likely than men to shift their emotional displays–this is probably more cultural than psychological in nature, though, as men are more socially constrained in the types of emotions they can display.

FACIAL REDDENING AND BLUSHING

We've spoken before about the "trauma of deceit" and how deception causes vast physiological changes with one's body. One of those changes can be a change in blood pressure that causes blood to suffuse the face, causing it to redden.

This response is more likely to be seen in lighter skin Caucasians than in other races, but can still be discerned in darker skin races.

The increase in blood pressure can also cause blood vessels to throb in the temples (just like strenuous exercise would). Some studies have actually shown that this increase in blood pressure can actually cause nasal tissue to expand—although this isn't visible to the naked eye. This increase in blood pressure can be seen from the base of the throat to the person's scalp in the form of blushing. (When I was a boy, my parents often joked that I could never hide anything from them because I blushed whenever I was embarrassed or stressed.) You may also notice veins standing out more prominently or even visibly throbbing in the person's temples and/or throat. This throbbing of the throat and facial veins was one of the signs I particularly watched for when I was a detective, particularly when it was a suspect who exhibited few other signs of deception.

Keep in mind that psychological stress is the cause of this physiological response and there can be other reasons than deception that cause this increase in blood pressure. The person could be embarrassed about being questioned or may just be very shy. As with any deception cue, this one must be evaluated in the context of the situation and in relation to any other cues being exhibited. In other words, an increase in blood pressure alone doesn't make one a liar. Interestingly, in my experience, females are most prone to exhibiting this deception cue.

ORIENTATION OF THE HEAD

In my research, I've encountered relatively little information about how liars position their heads during deceptive communication.

In one respect, this is a good thing, because it means you probably don't have any preconceived notions in place about how liars hold their heads.

Once again, I have to reinforce the need to carefully observe your subject when he is not lying and to get a baseline of his normal behavior. If you do not, you won't know which behaviors are indicative of deception.

In one of my favorite Westerns, a Texas Ranger faces five armed bad guys who are threatening to shoot him down. Four of the five are posturing, thumbing their guns, cursing and sneering; they **look** dangerous. The fifth bad guy, though, stands silently, just watching the lawman. When the lawman shoots this man, the others flee. When later asked why he shot the quiet one, the Ranger replied, "Because **he** was the **only** dangerous one."

Much like in that Western movie, the person who is lying to you is trying to control his behavior, but it's this rigid control that often gives him away. You may be inclined to think that someone who nods more or "twitches" is more likely to be a liar, but these are distractions—don't pay attention to them.

What you are looking for is a diminishment of movement, not an increase. Liars tend to so maintain such tight control of their body language that they are almost **too** conscious of it. This causes them to minimize their body language because they fear that their faces and movements will betray them. Liars may exhibit an unnatural stiffness in their head postures. This can even extend to their facial expressions, making a normally expressive person to seem stony-faced and impassive. When liars try to minimize "leakage" of their emotional and physio-logical arousal, they often over-do it. What they usually fail to realize, though, is that some leakage is almost impossible to prevent, which brings us to our next section, and one of the best indicators of deception.

MICRO-EXPRESSIONS

How many times have you listened to someone and thought, "God, this person is so-o-o-o-o stupid" and caught yourself rolling your eyes in disgust, even before you thought about it?

If you remember in the section about emotional displays, we discussed how facial displays of emotions precede verbal and physical reactions. Cops, for example, learn to watch suspects for the "target glance" which precedes a sucker punch or grab for the officer's handgun. But if more officers were trained to recognize micro-expressions, they could prevent far more attacks.

Micro-expressions are fleeting, momentary fragments of the emotions the person is truly feeling that flash oh-so-quickly across that person's face. This is part of the leakage that most people cannot control. Most people aren't even aware these micro-expressions exist or when they're exhibited on their faces.

Let's break down what happens.

You're taking with Jane and chatting about people you both know. You know Jane recently went on a date with another friend, Mark. You ask Jane how she liked the date with Mark, and Jane smiles and says she had a "good time." But if you'd examine her face more closely, though, you would have seen the faintest wrinkle of her nose and lifting of her upper lip.

- Were you to slow this expression down, you'd actually see that this is almost a full-blown expression of disgust! But because it occurs so quickly, most people don't even notice it.

- In this case, Jane didn't like **something** about the date or Mark himself, or both. Jane, not wanting to speak badly about a mutual friend, is controlling her emotions and reactions, but part of her true feelings leak out regardless of her intentions.

It takes some practice to recognize micro-expressions, but once you learn how to spot them, you'll find them to be one of the best indicators of deception. Micro-expressions occur so quickly and are often only partially formed, so people usually dismiss or don't even see them. Micro-expressions, however, give us a glimpse into what the person is truly feeling. Sometimes, this occurs before the person even realizes how they themselves feel the matter.

Think of it this way: If you touch a hot stove, your body reflexively back jerks your hand; it doesn't wait for your brain's intellectual side to compute the adverse effects of leaving your hand on the stove. But in jerking back your hand, you may knock over a stack of dishes at the same time. Obviously, given the opportunity, you would avoid knocking over those dishes, but your body doesn't allow the brain the time to "think" about the circumstances at hand—it just reacts to the stimuli.

Likewise, if you drink spoiled milk, you'll begin purging the bad milk from your system before your "thinking" brain realizes what's going on. Your sense of smell—which is responsible for your taste senses—will detect the spoiled milk and your gag reflex will kick in, preventing more from entering your system. You'll probably then expel the grotesque liquid from your mouth by spitting and/ or vomiting. But before any of that occurs, you'll form an expression of utter disgust on your face. Just as when you burned yourself on the hot stove, you'll probably form an expression of pain/shock/consternation on your face before you realize what's wrong!

Let's go back to that conversation with Jane about her date with Mark. What's happening in real time is this:

1. Jane hears your question.

2. The "reactive" part of Jane's brain recalls that Mark was a jerk and made a racist joke about another friend and upset Jane.

3. Jane's face begins to reflect her disgust at Mark's joke.

4. The thinking portion of Jane's brain begins to formulate a socially acceptable answer to your question, knowing that Mark is your friend too. Jane doesn't want to upset you …

5. Jane responds to your question while putting on a false smile, over-riding the still forming expression of disgust.

All of this happens in milliseconds as the civilized portion of Jane's brain exerts control over its emotional counter-part.

How often have you wanted to appear strong in the face of adversary, but felt tears forming in your eyes no matter how hard you wanted not to cry? Or tried to smile during a bad annual review at work, but felt your smile trembling on your face?

Other people fight to control their emotional states just as much as you, but it's not always a war that can be won. Stress (sometimes) causes our true emotions to surface even when we desperately want to hide them.

Micro-expressions don't always appear, but when they do, they are indicative of stronger, suppressed emotions. Many researchers believe that when a liar has something to lose that this is when micro-expressions and other leakage are most likely to manifest themselves. While I too believe this is true, I also believe strong primal emotions (like hate and fear) are more likely to "leak" when we try to hide them.

Don't mistake micro-expressions for facial tics or other involuntary facial movements. While facial tics and such can occur when a person is being deceptive, they are considered to be unreliable by the scientific community because they can be caused by so many different stimuli. Also, some studies suggest that people who have facial tics—much like people who stutter—actually have reduced incidences of their afflictions when lying!

In the next chapter, we'll look at the rest of Pinocchio's body and learn about some of the most frequently missed cues to deception.

Things to Remember

- The upper face more accurately shows the emotion a person is truly feeling.

- People who like you will usually raise their eyebrows when greeting you.

- Asymmetrical facial expressions are usually social masks designed to hide what a person is truly feeling.

- Liars tend to hold their heads straighter and minimize their movements.

- Micro-expressions are glimpses into how a person truly feels about the situation in which they find themselves.

5

Pinocchio's Upper Body and Limbs

She was practiced at the art of deception
Well I could tell by her blood-stained hands
        —The Rolling Stones, *You Can't Always Get What You Want*

We've already established that we miss over 50% of the lies blackest told to us—and that's when we're **expecting** someone to lie to us! The odds of us detecting deception decrease even more when we're expecting the truth from someone. One of the reasons we miss so many lies is that we look for the wrong cues; sometimes we look for cues (like eye movement) that aren't even associated with deception and, at other times, we look in the wrong places altogether!

We started Chapter Two by looking at Pinocchio's head not only because it's a natural place to do so, but because that's where most people look for deception cues. We focus most of our social interactions upon another person's face, but when it comes to detecting deception, we must look at **all** of Pinocchio's body. There is a wealth of nonverbal communication that goes on below Pinocchio's face ...

PINOCCHIO'S SHOULDERS

A particular phenomenon of body language that holds true across all cultures is that of shrugging—the lifting of our shoulders. Shrugging can mean several things: confusion, doubt, indecision, etc. If you ask someone directions to the bathrooms at a mall, and he hasn't been there before, he might shrug his shoulders and say, "I don't know." In this case, he's reinforcing his verbal message with a nonverbal message. The same thing might occur if a woman asks her husband where he wants to go to dinner: a verbal statement of "I don't care," combined with a noncommittal nonverbal message. But what if that same woman asks her husband if he'd like to go to Red Lobster for dinner, and he replies, "Sure!" followed by a shrug of his shoulders? Do you think he's really excited about going to Red Lobster, or do you think he'd rather go elsewhere?

Once again, I must remind you that nonverbal language is usually more indicative of the truth than anything someone says. We tend to very carefully monitor our words and how we say them, but we aren't as careful about our body language. And while we try to control our faces as much as possible, we are often very sloppy about controlling other parts of our body.

Shrugging is often a dead giveaway for even good liars.

I once interviewed a man accused of molesting a nine-year-old girl. When I asked him if there was any reason that anyone would say they saw him acting inappropriately around the girl, he first shrugged his shoulders, then he said, "No! I don't know why anyone would say that!" Obviously, his body language (shrugging) was incongruous with his flat denial. (He later confessed to sexually molesting the girl over a two year period.)

Sometimes, liars don't fully shrug their shoulders, but they engage in what Dr. Paul Ekman calls "micro-shrugs." These are very quick, but not fully developed shrugs, much like micro-expressions are fragmentary versions of full expressions.

When Pinocchio uses micro-shrugs, they will be very quick, jerky movements. They will most commonly occur when he voices a denial or states something in which he does not believe. Here again, the voice may shout one thing, but the body whispers another.

Micro-shrugs are one of the easiest pieces of body language to train someone to spot. This is because we tend to focus on the head and face area when communicating, and the shoulders are not far from that target area. Also, the eyes are predisposed to register motion, so the resulting twitches of a micro-shrug plays into our normal skill-set.

Here, though, is a recommendation when dealing with a person you suspect is being deceptive: Back off a step or two (especially if that person is a close or intimate friend).

We normally—during casual conversation—stay three to five feet away from one another. But if we are very comfortable with someone—or mad at someone!—we tend to move in closer to him. When comfortable, we allow people closer into our private spaces. And of course, the more aggressive of us tend to move closer toward people who are agitating us.

The problem, though, is that if we are too close, we cannot see all of Pinocchio's body and may miss out on some of his more "distant" body language. Many times, Pinocchio will be adept at hiding some aspects of his body language while being quite lousy at hiding other aspects, such as his arms and hands.

PINOCCHIO'S ARMS

Much has been written in body language books about "open" versus "closed" body language. There are many gurus out there that will tell you that people who have closed body language—arms crossed or held out in front of them to "block" the other person—are more likely to be deceptive than people with open body language. While there is a small element of truth to this belief, closed body language is meaningless **unless** Pinocchio's body language changes from open to closed in response to a **specific stimuli.** Even more importantly, the change can also be from closed to open; **what is truly important is the change itself.**

I once had a supervisor whose relaxed body language was keeping his arms and legs crossed, but if he was under pressure, he opened his body language. This made him very difficult to read in business meetings and depositions. When he testified in court, he was the picture of relaxation. When defense attorneys tried to rattle him, he just looked more relaxed and serene.

In many ways, his body language reflected that of a veteran poker player, whose body language is often reversed from that of the normal behavior exhibited by most people.

If you are a poker player and have wondered if there is general to follow when trying to determine if someone is bluffing, remember the rule of reversal: If someone acts confident, then he is probably holding a weak hand. If he acts hesitant, he probably holds a stronger hand. Professional poker players follow this rule when there are no other visible "tells" or other signs of deception. In poker and real life, though, there are other things to look for other than open or closed body language. For example:

- Liars show decreased use of illustrators—"talking" with one's arms and hands—than the honest. Therefore, if someone decreases his use of illustrators, you should immediately be suspicious.

- The use of adaptors may increase or decrease. Adaptors are those movements we make to sure our hair and clothing are in place. It is commonly thought that the use of adaptors is an indicator of deception, but this is not always true.

We often call these "nervous movements," but as we have already discussed, nervousness is not a reliable indicator of deception in and of itself alone.

• Liars often exhibit decreased overall arm and hand movement when lying. They tend to act stiffer and exercise more control over their muscular movements, and may grip the arms of a chair if sitting or hide their hands in their pockets. I've also seen obviously deceptive people sit on their hands in order to mask their mendacity.

Decreased arm and hand movements have been shown in numerous scientific studies to be a reliable indicator of deception. The reason this indicator appears to be valid is because while Pinocchio is constantly monitoring and editing his body language, he appears to exercise too much control.

Leakage of Pinocchio's true emotions, though, still may occur. Pinocchio may unconsciously clench his fists in anger or make obscene gestures and be totally unaware he is doing so.

PINOCCHIO'S HANDS

I interviewed a man who, when I asked him if he thought a rape victim "deserved it," curled up all the fingers of his right hand but the middle one—forming what I call the "Universal Sign of Contempt." He at first denied committing the rape, but later admitted to beating and raping the woman because she "led {him} on" by wearing provocative clothing.

Another sign of leakage is a slight outward movement of the hands. When we shrug, we often turn our hands upward and outward, so the palms face up. (Think of someone shrugging his shoulders while lifting his arms and palms up toward the sky.)

Just as in a micro-shrug, what we have here is someone who is exercising tremendous self-control, but he cannot effectively monitor everything, so slight twitches and spasms occur unbeknown to him. This leakage can occur anywhere—face, arms, or hands—and it can even shift the area in which it occurs. What seems to happen is that when Pinocchio concentrates on controlling one aspect of his body language, he loses control of other components of his presentation. In effect, there is simply too much for Pinocchio to effectively monitor.

Many times, Pinocchio may present a calm and controlled appearance, but he may be clenching his fists in rage. I've seen Pinocchio clench his fists so hard that his fingernails puncture the skin of his palms, causing blood to drip onto the floor of my office. Yet, all the while, he continued smiling that fake social smile and pretended to be innocent, cooperative, and unafraid. You should also be wary if Pinocchio starts cracking his knuckles when you ask relevant questions and ask yourself why he is releasing stress at that particular time.

SPECIFIC BEHAVIORS

When you are speaking with Pinocchio, there are some gestures and behaviors that have more importance than others:

1. Steepling or "tenting" of the fingers. This can mean Pinocchio is very confident of his position at the moment. It can also mean he is disregarding everything you are saying to him. This is a gesture that is used most frequently by powerful people (or people who believe they are powerful), and extroverts are more likely to exhibit this gesture than introverts.

2. Spidering of the fingertips. This is when Pinocchio's hands are palm-down on a surface but the hand is not flat. Instead, his fingertips are positioned so they look like he is getting ready to dig into the table or other surface. This gesture indicates Pinocchio is impatient and wants to say something. It can also mean he is anxious to leave.

3. Clenching of the fist(s). This gesture can indicate anger, aggression, or excitement.

4. Palms facing up. This is often called the "believe me" posture. It is typically used by very good liars in an attempt to portray honesty. The difference between the use of this gesture by the dishonest versus the honest is the length of time it is used—liars tend to hold the gesture longer—and its stiffness. Honest people tend to have very relaxed hands with slightly curled fingers when using this gesture; Pinocchio, though, tends to be very stiff with fully extended fingers. When Pinocchio uses this gesture, his stiffness usually makes the gesture seem artificial.

5. Brushing movements away from the body. This is a dismissive behavior and is indicative of Pinocchio's attitude toward you.

The main thing to watch for when observing the hands is to compare Pinocchio's words to the body language being exhibited. Pinocchio's hands can betray him despite his best efforts to control all other aspects of his verbal message.

PINOCCHIO'S TRUNK

Another often-overlooked portion of Pinocchio's body is the chest. Specifically, there are two aspects of the trunk to monitor:

1. Posture. Liars tend to maintain a stiffer posture and exhibit fewer postural shifts when dissembling. This plays into the general theme of Pinocchio attempting to over-control his body language. Some liars have also been shown to engage less in forward leaning than the truthful. There is a debate as to why this is so; one school of thought believes it's because liars don't want to be closely observed, but another thinks that this is a mannerism exhibited mostly by introverted liars and less so by extroverted liars.

2. Alignment. The deceptive change their bodily alignment less often than the truthful, but here again this is some debate in regard to personality types. Studies have shown that extroverted liars tend to "lock onto" their targets, just as they tend to engage in more direct gazing than the truthful. Introverts, though, tend to angle themselves slightly away, as if seeking an escape route.

While introverted and extroverted personality types may show differences in how they practice deception, the main thing to remember is that both may over-control their postures and bodily alignments. While the truthful will show fluidity and move around to become comfortable, the deceptive are less likely to do so.

Again, we must remain aware that we are looking for **changes** in our subject's normative behavior. Just because someone sits or stands ramrod straight and does not move around much does not necessarily mean he is being deceptive. He could be a military veteran or have back problems.

I once worked with a jury consultant who told me that he thought a perspective jury member was unsociable because he leaned away from the other jury members when sitting. After watching the man's interactions with his peers, I disagreed. When the jury pool returned to room after the break, the man sat in a different seat on the other side of the room, and was now leaning toward the jury. It turned out that the man had an old war injury that caused him discomfort when he sat in any other way.

If you want to see a true example of bodily alignment, watch the *Dr. Phil Show* and observe the host's body language and that of his guests. Whenever Phil disagrees with a guest, he tends to lean away from that guest while listening to him. And if a couple experiencing marital problems is on the show, they tend to lean away from each other when discussing their issues—even if they're holding hands at the time. The problem with learning a little about body language is that we tend to over analyze people without regard to their individual characteristics. Every interaction brings with it a unique set of circumstances and may be affected by sexual roles, societal status and other stressors.

I once attended a series of law enforcement interrogation training courses, and as a matter of course, one often sees the same people over and over again at such seminars. At one seminar, an acquaintance told a very humorous story about a stopping a woman dressed as a clown (she was in full-face paint, no less!) and the difficulty he had proving the woman's identity … the story was a huge hit.

A month later, I attended the advanced course, and again, my acquaintance told the same story. This time, though, his body language and presentation were markedly different. One other attendant remarked in private that he thought the story wasn't true, I didn't think he was being deceptive, but something was amiss. What had changed?

Later on, I discovered the reason for the acquaintance's unease and poor delivery. It seems that he had developed a crush on a certain female detective who was at the second seminar, and this normally confident and articulate man turned into a blithering idiot every time this woman stood near him!

This was a classic case of someone mistaking social anxiety for deception—something even the experts can sometimes do.

Even the most confident of us fall prey to social anxiety and sexual tensions from time to time. Because of this compounding factor, law enforcement officers who are knowledgeable in the science of interrogation strive to create as neutral an environment as possible. Interrogations are conducted one on one—that way, the interpersonal dynamics are muted—and distractions such as telephones are removed from the interrogation room. Even the paint schemes are designed to be calming and subdued.

The lesson I wish you to take from this is to be wary of making judgments regarding honesty when people are in groups. It's simply too hard to separate truthful behavior from its deceptive counterpart due to all the attendant social and group dynamics.

Pinocchio's Legs and Feet

Due to my experience conducting interrogations, I've had much experience watching both honest and dishonest people plead their innocence in what is often an unforgiving environment: the interrogation room.

When I first became a detective, I read everything I could about body language. While I found a lot had been written about the upper body (true or false), relatively little in the literature addressed the legs and feet. I believe this to be a mistake, but an understandable one; after all, most interrogators used to sit across desks from their suspects and the lower limbs were not readily observable.

It was not until recently that interrogators were taught to remove desks and tables from the interrogation room. Modernly trained interrogators sit with no physical or psychological barriers between them and their suspects, and this has allowed many new observations to be made regarding Pinocchio's lower body.

The first observation I will impart to you is that the stiffness and minimization of movement normally associated with Pinocchio's upper body does not seem to apply as much to his lower limbs. Curiously, while Pinocchio takes great care to monitor his upper body, he does not seem to monitor his lower body as much. This does not mean that liars totally disregard their legs and feet, but the same standard of care doesn't always apply. An observant person can notice quite a bit of leakage by watching Pinocchio's lower limbs.

The only problem this leakage is that it's often non-specific; while one can often tell what emotion Pinocchio is hiding by observing other parts of his body, this is not usually the case with the legs and feet.

There are two notable exceptions to this maxim: Aggression and fear.

I have seen cases where people have literally been pantomiming snap kicks at their interviewers. In business meetings, I've also seen seemingly perfectly composed executives kicking away at board members, as well as subordinates angrily stomping the floor while smiling and nodding at their bosses.

On the other end of the emotional spectrum—the one occupied by fear—I've known people to literally run in place (all the while sitting and going nowhere).

Of course, much of the time, Pinocchio's leg movements are simply the release of pent-up stress, anxiety and boredom.

Any good college professor can tell when his students are ready to leave after a long lecture (as if the packing of books and rattling of keys aren't enough), because the vast sea of feet start angling toward the door. Likewise, if you are talking with someone and she begins to angle her feet away from you, she is signaling that your conversation/chance of getting a date/likelihood of getting her phone number is about to end!

If Pinocchio is showing signs of aggression or a desire to flee your presence, you have to ask yourself why he is feeling those emotions. If he is professing his love for you, but is "kicking" you all the while he is mouthing the words, I'd tend believe his actions rather than his words.

The same goes for someone whom claims he wants to talk to you, but sits or stands with his feet angled toward the nearest exit. This lack of frontal alignment may be accompanied by the raising of one or both of his heels—a micro-run, if you will! Obviously, a cooperative person will want to stay and talk once you gain his confidence and he reaches a minimum level of comfort. But someone who is signaling a desire to flee is usually withholding information and is inclined to be deceptive.

Here is another reason why watching Pinocchio's lower limbs will help you: While a very skilled liar may be successful in disguising his deceptive body language—after all, some would-be liars will be bound to buy this and other books to pick up pointers—there is usually some leakage somewhere. You just have to be looking in the proper place at the proper time. Sometimes, that tremor in Pinocchio's legs will be the first betrayal you'll observe in an otherwise icy exterior. By itself, it's not a firm indication of deception, but if it occurs when you ask a very pointed question, then you have a specific response linked to a specific stimuli. Once you find that you can spot one indicator of deception, you should find that it gives you more confidence in spotting other signs.

Too often, even law enforcement officers ask a few questions and then give up when they get a few denials. I was often asked to re-interview suspects that other officers claimed "would never confess," and I got confessions in a majority of those interviews. The reason I was successful in those cases is because I was able to spot the hidden indicators of deception, which gave me the confidence that we had the right person. After that, it became a case of who would give up first: he or me.

The last item of interest is Pinocchio's stance. A wide stance generally denotes confidence in a situation, while legs that are closer together than shoulder-width indicates the opposite. This may be related to the flight-versus-fight reaction. A body that isn't in a wide stance can quickly shift into a run, etc., whereas a person who is relaxed and has a wide stance is slower to react to a threat.

In the next chapter, we'll discuss what to do and say once you think Pinocchio is lying to you. In other words, how to get the truth out of him!

Things to Remember

- Shrugs and micro-shrugs are often coupled with deceptive statements.

- You should stand back slightly in order to see all of Pinocchio's body language.

- Liars show decreased use of illustrators and adapters.

- Liars show decreased adjustments in posture and frontal alignment.

- Don't try to determine truthfulness in a group setting. One-on-one is usually the best method of limiting distractions. One must account for social and sexual roles in order to separate deceptive behavior from mere social anxiety.

- Watch the legs and feet. Is Pinocchio exhibiting aggression, fear or a desire to flee?

6

Getting the Truth

Now you say your trust's getting weaker
Probably coz my lies just started getting deeper

—The Black Eye Peas, *Don't Lie*

While becoming a skilled reader of body language will undoubtedly help you in your day-to-day life, there are times when you'll need to get Pinocchio to admit he is lying. It may be that you're a law enforcement officer, corporate loss prevention investigator or small business owner who needs a confession to take the next step in your investigation.

Or maybe—just maybe—you're a jilted lover who needs to hear the confession from Pinocchio's lying mouth before you'll believe you've been cheating on?

In many ways, the confession is the proof of the pudding. No matter how much evidence we may have that Pinocchio is lying, it's the confession we want (and sometimes need) to hear.

I've had personal experience with this myself. Many times, I knew someone was lying to me when I was a police officer, but no matter how much proof I had on Pinocchio—be it fingerprints, forensic evidence, or eyewitness testimony—the State Attorney's office would want to know if I had gotten a confession. If I had a confession, I had no problem getting the attorneys onboard; if I didn't, they always seemed to want more proof before they'd move ahead with prosecuting Pinocchio.

I've seen the same thing time and again in the corporate world with thieves and embezzlers. I've actually had cases where employees were caught stealing on videotape and still had problems getting everyone to agree to fire (let's not even discuss prosecuting!) the offender.

It's really no surprise, after all, that the *Jerry Springer Show* can run that same "special" on cheating spouses being hooked up to polygraphs to "reveal the truth" about their infidelity. Jilted lovers, assistant state attorneys, corporate officers and the rest of us always want to hear the guilty parties confess to their sins.

Take the case of O.J. Simpson. Here is a man whose blood and DNA were found at the scene of his wife's murder! One would think that the criminal trial would have been an open and shut case, but what it lacked, of course, was the one thing the jury wanted to hear: OJ admitting to committing the murders. Of course, he was found guilty in the civil trial, but that isn't the point. The Simpson defense team did an absolutely brilliant job of placing reasonable doubt in the jury's mind during the criminal trial, while the prosecution simply missed the boat.

Had OJ confessed to those murders, my opinion is that the defense would have run several "mock trials" before the actual trial, and OJ's lawyers would have conceded that a plea bargain would have been their best option. As it was, they played a very well-run game of ignoring the evidence and attacking the credibility of the experts.

Could the Simpson trial have turned out differently? The evidence suggests it might have if the detectives who interviewed OJ had conducted the interview differently.

Here's what I mean:

When LAPD detectives Tom Lange and Phil Vannatter interviewed OJ Simpson, they asked him questions about where he was and what he was doing at the time of the murders, as well as established OJ's rocky marital status and history of domestic violence. They even ventured (albeit poorly) into the fact that Simpson had a cut on his hand, and that his blood may be at the crime scene (it was all over his house and inside his Bronco).

But they never, ever gave OJ a chance to confess ...

The interview was conducted for a scant 32 minutes. Not only was that a remarkably short time for a homicide interview, but there appeared to be no psychological stratagem considered or employed to induce OJ to confess. It is one of the worst interviews I've ever analyzed.

First, we need to understand is that no one confesses without having or being given a reason to do so. Even those people who walk into a police station and confess to having murdered someone do so for a reason. It could be they are experiencing overwhelming guilt and confessing makes them feel better; in some cases, it's because they want the attention confessing will bring them. In fact, any sensational homicide will usually have at least one person confess to the crime who had absolutely nothing to do with it—these are the people who want the "status" of being known as murderers but don't want to do the killing(s) themselves.

But there has to be some incentive for exposing oneself to punishment and/or adverse consequences. Without that incentive, there is no reason to confess.

Secondly, Pinocchio must **believe** you know he is lying. If he doesn't think he has been caught, then there is no reason to confess. There has to be an implication that you already know and can "prove" Pinocchio is guilty—even though you may not truly know he has lied and haven't a shred of proof.

What skilled interrogators do is weave "proof of guilt" and an incentive to confess into a net that makes Pinocchio believe he has been caught, and that his only way out is to confess.

I know that it sounds improbable that someone would confess to something you have no real proof he's done, but it occurs every day in interrogation rooms across our nation.

I have personally interviewed people who I've had no proof committed a crime and obtained confession after confession. Of course, I suspected they committed those crimes, but without their willing cooperation, I would never have been able to prove their guilt. There are literally hundreds of people sitting in jail cells at this moment for crimes ranging from theft to homicide simply because I was able to convince them to spill their secrets.

If I can convince someone to sell me his very freedom, you can convince your lover to tell you about cheating on you or your boss to reveal whether you are getting that raise you deserve.

It shouldn't come as a great revelation that no one wants to be labeled as a no good son of a bitch. Most of us, though, when we set out to discover the truth, do exactly that! We not only want the truth, but we also want to point out to Pinocchio that he's lower than whale scum.

In short, we almost make it impossible for Pinocchio to come clean.

I once worked with an officer who named Tony who had arrested a well-known thief for possession of a stolen bicycle. The bicycle had been taken in burglary that involved the burglary of an elderly couple's home. While the possession of the bicycle wasn't enough to arrest this cretin for the home's invasion, it was certainly a reason to look closely at him.

Tony tried to interview the young man (whom I'll call Freddie), but he had no success. As the department's head investigative interviewer, Tony called me. When I walked into the squad room, Tony's face was inches from Freddie's. Tony was screaming at Freddie, "Do you think it's right to break into someone's home?"

Freddie was an old hand at being yelled at by cops. He knew that, eventually, cops get tired of yelling and then take you to jail. After a few hours in jail, he'd walk free. (Bicycle theft is not considered very important in the criminal justice community.)

The first thing I did was take Freddie someplace private where we wouldn't be interrupted. In this case, it was an interrogation room equipped with two chairs and nothing else.

It took three hours of talking, but eventually, Freddie confessed to burglarizing seven homes and provided property that he'd taken from each of them. We started out talking about his family, the people we both knew, and how badly Tony had treated Freddie. The whole effort behind the first hour was to talk about everything **but** the crime. While that may seem strange to you, it gave me the opportunity to get acquainted with Freddie's baseline body language and to ease his apprehension. I wanted Freddie to be as comfortable as possible, and to then ease him into my trap.

After I established rapport with Freddie—he was actually laughing at one point—we started to discuss **why** he was in the interview room with me. Certainly, we both **knew** why we were there, but like a customer and a salesman negotiating a car's price, we were negotiating how much information Freddie was going to give me.

The next thing I did was to determine if Freddie had committed the crime. The first piece of evidence, of course, was that Freddie had a bicycle taken from the scene of the crime. But stolen bicycles frequently trade hands on the streets—sometimes several times within hours of being stolen—so the possession of the bicycle was only circumstantial. So I conducted what is called by some interrogation schools a "Behavioral Analysis Interview," and others a "Cognitively Anchored Interview." The end result is the same: Liars, as we have discussed, speak and act markedly different than honest people. Here is a list of questions I asked Freddie, along with the way an innocent should answer (for brevity, I'm not detailing his body language):

1. Freddie, do you know why I asked you here today?
    Answer: "No." (Innocent people do not evade the issue, as both of you know why you are there.)

2. Freddie, we are investigating a burglary, let me ask you right up front: Did you do this? Answer: (long pause) "No I did not." (Remember what we discussed about contractions and time-buying mechanisms?)

3. Freddie, do you know who did this?
    Answer: "Anybody could've done it." (Innocent people will generally offer somebody specific. Guilty suspects do not want to identify anyone, as this would narrow the focus of the investigation.)

4. Freddie, is there anyone you would say did not do this?
    Answer: "I only know about me." (Most innocent people will vouch for someone. Guilty suspects will often say they can "only vouch for themselves.")

5. Freddie, how do you feel about being interviewed about this thing?
    Answer: "It's bullshit. Someone gave me that bike and I ain't done nothing." (Innocent people usually do not act angrily or negative.)

6. Freddie, do you think that this really happened, or do you think something else is going on?
    Answer: "They be white people. They probably got big-time insurance." (Innocent people will affirm that this crime actually occurred. Guilty suspects often say that the crime did not occur.)

7. Freddie, who do you think would have the best opportunity to do this thing?
    Answer: "Don't know. Someone else." (Guilty suspects will often refuse to name someone, or they suggest a different person than they did in question number three.)

8. Freddie, why do you think someone would do this?
    Answer: "Maybe he needed the money." (Innocent people will usually call the perpetrator a criminal or sick.)

9. Freddie, did you ever think of doing something like this?
    Answer: "Yeah."(Innocent people usually say they have not. Guilty suspects often say they have thought of committing such crimes.)
    Freddie, what do you think should happen to the person who did this
    Answer: "Get a warning." (Innocent people will suggest an appropriate punishment.)

10. Freddie, how do you think the results of this investigation will turn out on you?
    Answer: "I dunno." (Innocent people will be confident and say they will be absolved.)

11. Freddie, do you think these people caused this thing to happen, even slightly?
   Answer: "Yeah. They should've locked up their shit. They done be living here long enough." (Innocent people will not blame a victim for the crime.)

12. Freddie, do think the person who did this deserves a second chance?
   Answer: "Yeah. Everybody makes mistakes. Like if it's his first time or needs money, you know, cause people need stuff." (Innocent people will usually reject the idea of a second chance.)

13. Freddie, would you be willing to take a polygraph test?
   Answer: (Long pause) "I dunno." (Innocent people usually do not hesitate at all in answering affirmatively. Guilty suspects often hesitate, even if they agree to such.)

14. Freddie, how do you think you'd do on that lie detector test?
   Answer: (Longer pause) "I dunno." (Innocent people do not hesitate to say they would pass such a test. Guilty suspects express doubts about passing.)

15. Freddie, is there any reason that are investigation would show that someone saw you at the scene of the crime?
   Answer: (Long pause) "Maybe I walked by there or something.
   (Innocent people will make a firm, immediate denial.)
   This last question is referred to as the Bait Question.

It's designed to make the suspect believe there is evidence against him and to weaken his resolve. You will most often see a deceptive or guilty suspect exhibit his greatest amount of stress when answering this question.

Since Freddie's responses and his body language showed he was being deceptive, I went onto the next stage of the interview. I exited the room and came back in a few minutes later accompanied by a department secretary. I had Freddie stand up, and said to the secretary, "Is this him?"

The secretary nodded and walked out of the room. (Note: The secretary was accustomed to this game and had never seen Freddie before!) I then came back in a few minutes later holding a file folder that had Freddie's name printed in large block letters across it. The folder was impressively filled with papers, one of which was entitled *Witness Statement* (and was poking conveniently outside the folder where Freddie could see it). I stood in front of Freddie and said, "Freddie, our investigation clearly shows you committed this crime. Now we need to talk."

At this point, Freddie certainly thought we had a mountain of evidence against him, including an eyewitness. But enticing Freddie to confess required more than making him think we had him cold; as I've said, people need an **incentive** to admit to their deception. Freddie was an old hand at this game, and now I needed to convince him that confessing was in his best interests.

If you remember Chapter One, we discussed some of the reasons why people tell lies. In Freddie's case, he was lying for self-protection—he didn't want to go to jail—so my main battle was getting him over that fear.

Stan Walters, one of my contemporaries and a well-known expert on deception, agrees with me that almost everything said in an interview is important. In Freddie's case, Freddie himself gave me the keys I needed to unlock his confession. Think of the things he said:

1. The victims are white and have "big time" insurance. They probably didn't suffer much of financial loss.

2. The victims contributed to the loss by not locking up their house better.

3. Freddie tacitly asked for a "second chance" and implied he needed money.

What I did next was feed those same reasons back to Freddie. I told him that sometimes we all get into trouble sometimes, and anyone who says they haven't stolen something at least once in their lives is a liar! And if someone was hungry or needed to get money for his family, then sometimes stealing is understandable.

But the big difference, I told Freddie, is that good people admit when they make mistakes. After all, whom would you rather deal with: A person who admits he made a mistake or someone who is just a thief?

The answer was obvious: Freddie thought he'd rather deal with someone who "made a mistake."

I continued with the theme that someone who simply made a mistake is different from a "bad person," particularly if that mistake was made to help support his family. And really, no one was truly hurt, because the people whose stuff had been "borrowed" had insurance, right?

When Freddie began nodding and hanging his head, it was time for the next step: offering Freddie a "good" reason for committing the crime versus a "bad" reason. I asked Freddie, "Did you do this because you needed to get money for your family, or because you're a drug addict?"

Freddie's reply? "For my family."

The rest of the discussion was just getting the full details of his confession ...

There are a lot of roads and techniques to get to this same place (the confession), and we're now going to discuss more of them. I'll give you a basic formula upon which you can build your techniques.

STEP ONE: TALK ALONE

Never confront Pinocchio in a group setting if at all possible. The psychological pressure to **not** confess is simply too immense. Think of time when you had a secret; maybe had **done** something you shouldn't have done, or perhaps you **wanted** to do something you thought others might not approve of you doing. If you told someone about your actions—past or future—did you tell a group of people, or just one person?

We tend to share secrets only with a select few people in our lives. Sometimes, it's with several people, but on an individual basis. Rarely do we shout our deepest, darkest sins the whole world—unless you're on the *Jerry Springer* show, of course!

Think of Pinocchio's confessions in the same manner. When and if he does confess, he needs privacy and the perception that he isn't going to be embarrassed in front of the whole world.

Even if you can't be totally alone, get Pinocchio off to the side somewhere. When I was a detective, my partner and I often had problems interviewing suspects because other officers and staff would barge into our cubicles and interrupt our interrogations. Our solution to this particular problem was to find two old doors at a yard sale and mount them to our cubicle entrances along with signs that said, "Interview in Progress. Don't Disturb."

Although everyone could still hear our entire conversation, it gave our suspects the illusion of privacy, and our confession rates shot up dramatically. Even though our sergeant, Steve, could easily peer over the sides of my cubicle, the suspects felt they had more privacy because they couldn't see anyone but me. (Steve was fond of dangling notes over some suspects' heads that said things like, "Ask him about the burglary on West Euclid Avenue." Luckily, they never saw him do that!)

If you are a law enforcement officer, private detective or retail investigator who conducts interviews, you should make it absolutely clear to your fellow workers and support staff that your interviews should never be interrupted. We had a secretary in our Criminal Investigation Division who had worked for the department forever, and she could never absorb that concept. Every phone call and message was of the uttermost importance to her, and it didn't matter if I was conducting a homicide interview, she was going to deliver that message. People like that will screw up an interview in a heartbeat, and sometimes—as in this particular secretary's case—they'll do it on purpose. Getting Pinocchio to confess is like walking a tightrope; if the flow of conversation is disturbed, you may have to regain your equilibrium and start over again. Or you may fail completely and lose the chance forever.

STEP TWO: ESTABLISH RAPPORT

Early in my law enforcement career, I attended a seminar entitled Advanced Interrogation Techniques conducted by Elmhurst (IL) Police Chief John Milner, who taught us a very simple lesson: People like people who most similar to themselves.

Milner taught us to learn everything possible about our suspects and to use that knowledge to pretend to be "clones" of that person. The theory is that the more perceived points of similarity there are between an interviewer and his suspect, the more likely the interviewer is to get a confession. Research has since proven Milner's theory to be correct. People naturally gravitate toward those who are similar to themselves in looks, opinions and social status.

Building on that principle, I learned to masquerade as everything from a beach bum to a pedophile …

I would learn what type of women Pinocchio liked and before he arrived in my office, I'd have its walls festooned pictures of blondes, brunettes, redheads—whatever his favorite "flavor" happened to be. I'd even bought surfboards (I knew absolutely nothing about surfing prior to assuming that new role, but a visit to the library brought me up to speed) and hung them on my walls in order to discuss surfing with one guy.

If my target were a racist, I'd admit to agreeing with his position; if he were a pedophile, I'd remark on the attractiveness of little kids in magazines I'd have laid out on my desk. I'd even study the neighborhoods that my suspects grew up in so that I could at least pretend to have visited them before. My supervisor used to be driven nuts by the amount of preparation I would make prior to a major interview, but it almost always paid off.

Before Pinocchio walked into my office, I knew everything I could about him, and I used that knowledge to start a conversation that **he** would be interested in, not **me**. In other words, I talked about him, not me, not the case. We are usually the thing in which we are most interested and are often self-absorbed, selfish creatures.

There's another maxim that Milner taught me, and it's this: Once people start talking, it's hard for them to stop.

I'd spend over an hour or more at times discussing old cars, motorcycles, fly-fishing, and almost anything else you can think of. I once had a three hour discussion about the old Dark Shadows series because the woman I was interviewing was a science fiction fanatic! Once we were rocking and rolling along, I'd switch gears and start into the real interview. And in most cases, people never knew what hit them. Suddenly, their newly found friend became their closest confidant.

Like I said, once people begin talking, it's hard for them to stop.

Establishing rapport can mean different things in different settings and relationships, though. If you're already someone's friend, lover, boyfriend, girlfriend or spouse, then you **already** have rapport established. All you need to do is reinforce it! In those situations, all you need do is talk about past good times that you've had together—just get those good memories flowing! Let me state this unequivocally: Everyone—even the most murderous, sociopathic S.O.B.—wants to connect with other people. You just have to find the right wavelength. Hitler, Saddam Hussein, Mussolini, and even Ted Bundy had people in their lives with whom they shared their secrets.

If you're dealing with a stranger with whom you've had little or no contact—like a used car salesman—than look at his desk or what he's wearing. Does he have a picture of his boat, family, or other trinkets that give you some insight into his psyche? How about a high school or college ring? If you can get Pinocchio to talk about himself, you've established rapport. **People love to talk about themselves!** Once he begins talking about one thing, it'll be easier to get him to talk about the topic in which **you're** really interested. Another technique you can use to assist you in gaining rapport is to **SOFTEN** up Pinocchio throughout the interview.

STEP THREE: USING THE S.O.F.T.E.N. TECHNIQUE

SOFTEN is an acronym that stands for:

- **S**mile. Smiling shows friendliness and a willingness to listen. It makes you seem nonjudgmental.

- **O**pen gestures. Using open gestures shows you're open and approachable. Talk with your hands; it makes you a more engaging and captivating speaker.

- **F**orward leaning. Leaning toward Pinocchio closes the interpersonal distance and makes the conversation more intimate. Studies show that the closer you stand to Pinocchio, the more rapport he will feel with you.

- **T**ouch. Appropriate touching (on Pinocchio's hands or arms) also helps to establish rapport.

- **E**yebrows raised. Raising your eyebrows when greeting Pinocchio and during the conversation reinforces the rapport you've established. When Pinocchio says something with which you agree, raising your eyebrows encourages him to continue. You can also use this technique to encourage Pinocchio to continue talking when his conversation trails off; this allows you to state nonverbally, "Go on, I'm listening …" This is often better than saying anything at all and is called the Pregnant Silence Technique.

- **N**od. Nodding throughout the conversation—particularly when Pinocchio starts to confess—helps him continue to speak. It's rewarding and an affirmation that he's doing the right thing.

Once you've established rapport, it's time to shift gears and focus upon the real reason for being there. In order to get Pinocchio's confession, of course, you'll have to convince him of three things:

1. You know the truth.

2. You understand why he did what he did …

3. Telling the truth has greater rewards than continuing to lie.

STEP FOUR: DETERMINE IF PINOCCHIO IS LYING

You'll need to ask Pinocchio the same type of questions that I asked Freddie about the burglary he committed. Remember: Liars minimize, give excuses for bad acts, blame victims and otherwise justify their acts. We've also learned that liars have chronological differences in the way they relate their stories compared to the truthful, as well as exhibiting different body language.

When asking Pinocchio your questions, you will need to ask several questions to determine if he is being dishonest. You cannot determine honesty within only a few questions, and when you are evaluating his behavior, you have a lot of observing to do. Nor do you have to ask your questions one after another; it's often easier to incorporate the questions into normal conversation (such as when talking to a colleague over lunch or a car salesperson across the negotiation table). You must tailor your questions to the environment in which you will be operating.

Although my background is that of a police detective, I certainly cannot approach every person I suspect of being deceptive like I'm walking into an interrogation room. Still, you must have a game plan. Determine which questions you will ask in advance and how many you will ask. Just because you have 10 questions in mind doesn't mean you must ask all of them; if you determine Pinocchio is dishonest by asking five questions, you might want to move on to the next step. Ask as many questions as needed to make your determination, but I suggest asking no less than five of those questions.

Likewise, if you determine that Pinocchio is being honest, then there is no reason to move forward to the next step. While this may seem like common sense, there is a great tendency for people to ignore the evidence that someone is being honest and push forward in an attempt to get a confession. If you think it doesn't happen, then you aren't recalling the Central Park Jogger case and every other false confession the police have psychologically coerced out of innocent people.

The Innocence Project, established in 1992 and dedicated to exonerating the innocent through post-conviction DNA testing, has since its inception, proven the innocence of more than 170 people, including 14 who were at one time sentenced to death. A significant portion of those cases involve false confessions, in addition to mistaken eyewitness identifications and other bad information. Don't let your emotions over-rule your objectivity. It can be hard—particularly if you're emotionally invested in the outcome. One of the biggest problems in law enforcement interrogations is that cops not only get convinced of someone's guilt (and more rarely, innocence) and refuse to quit until they get what they want. Even worse, cops are pushed to get results by their political handlers (who have no patience for the length of time needed to conduct a proper investigation).

STEP FIVE: CONVINCING PINOCCHIO YOU KNOW THE TRUTH

Before you switch gears and begin to interview Pinocchio, you must realize he has probably already committed to a defensive posture in his mind. Think of it this way: Whenever he committed whatever act he is lying about, he knew he could get caught and thought up at least some of his lies in advance. Let's discuss alibis for a moment and I'll explain why they're nothing to be concerned about. In fact, let's view Pinocchio's preparations by putting yourself in his place for a moment:

Let's say you've been caught driving drunk. When the officer pulled you over, you probably were already working on a series of lies to get yourself out of a ticket or an arrest. Perhaps it's the minimization story: "I only had one beer; that's why my breath smells of alcoholic beverages."

Now, if you're pulled over by an inexperienced cop, that story might work. But frankly, most cops wouldn't believe you. You simply haven't put enough forethought into your lying. You're probably going to jail unless you can successfully play upon the officer's sympathies …

But if you're a more experienced drunk, you may have a bottle of mouthwash in your glove box and maybe even eye drops in there. You'll not admit to drinking at all and may say that you're feeling a little ill—hence the erratic driving. If you're very clever, you'll decline to take any of those pesky field sobriety tests (after all, you're **sick**, not drunk!) and ask the officer to call someone to take you home.

In the second scenario, you stand a much greater chance of not being arrested. You've actually done some pre-planning and your deception is smoothly scripted.

But it's still scripted, and since it's not the truth, you'd have to improvise if the cop starts poking holes in your story. How long have you been sick? Where are you coming from at 2 a.m.? Suppose the cop calls the closest bar and asks if you were there that night? Or even worse, suppose you're with a buddy who isn't as glib, and the cop takes him aside and asks him questions about your night on the town? What if your wife arrives and starts contradicting your story, stating this is the third time you've been pulled over that month?

Your entire story could unravel with just a few pulls here and there by an astute interviewer … all he would need is to find a few loose threads in your web of deception.

Your job when interviewing Pinocchio is to start pulling on those loose threads if Pinocchio comes up with an alibi. People tend to worry about alibis a lot more than is warranted. I've only had a few occasions in which Pinocchio has come up with a worthwhile alibi, and each time, Pinocchio's alibi fell apart once we started talking. The secret, of course, is to get and keep him talking!

To convince Pinocchio you already know most or all of the truth, all you must do is put a seed of doubt in his mind by implying you have some evidence of his guilt—whether you have such evidence or not. Here are some of the techniques I've successfully used in the past:

1. Fake witnesses. I've had secretaries walk into a room, look at a suspect for a few seconds, nod in an exaggerated manner to me and then walk back out. In this manner, I've implied Pinocchio has been identified and never even had to say a word about a witness to him.

2. Cameras. My friends, cameras are everywhere these days. Last weekend, I noticed that even the intersection near my house now has one. Almost all major retailers, including convenience stores and mall parking lets, are electronically monitored. I've implied to Pinocchio many times that I've had video footage of him either committing crimes or being where he is not supposed to be. Think of it this way: if you were to consider all the video cameras at your local grocery store, Blockbuster™ video, Dominos Pizza™, and traffic intersections—say, within a 10 mile radius from your home—how many times do you think you'd be on camera? How much would it take to convince your curfew-violating son or daughter that due to video cameras that you know he or she was out past that curfew?

3. Cellular phone records. One of the facts of life in the electronic age is that we are tracked almost constantly. For instance, many cell phones store at least the last 10 phone numbers that were received by or dialed from that phone. Those same phones can also act as GPS devices—whether or not they are GPS capable—and can tell you where the phone is located (even if turned off). Think of how Pinocchio's mind will be spinning if you walk into a room while holding his phone and state, "We need to talk about something …"

4. FLURB (Fluoroscopic Lymphatic Un-sequenced Byproducts). Almost everyone knows about fingerprints and DNA, but few people understand the concept of FLURB. FLURB are those particles of skin containing DNA, trace elements, and oils that we constantly shed. I once had a partner who was so good at detecting FLURB that he could tell by sniffing the air—with-

out any equipment, mind you!—if you had been in a particular room. The best example of FLURB, though, is how police canines and blood hounds track humans. If dogs relied strictly upon skin particles to follow a trail, of course, they would quickly lose the trail because skin flakes are so small and light that they blow all over the place. FLURB, however, is composed of so many elements and oils that it is difficult to disperse or destroy (you've probably seen the crime show CSI: Miami where they've used small vacuums to pick up FLURB elements at crime scenes). All one needs to do is compare the FLURB found on an object to a person's FLURB by mixing both samples with three teaspoons of white vinegar to separate the oils. If the vinegar becomes pink colored when combined, then the test is positive and you have a match.

5. Paper trails. From credit cards to electronic toll records, people leave a trail wherever they go. Not only can you imply you have evidence of Pinocchio's whereabouts and travels, but in many cases, you can find actual evidence.

6. The file folder. A scene from the Matrix could have been taken from any number of my interviews. The bad guy, Mr. Smith, walks into the interrogation room where NEO (Keanu Reeves) is sitting. Smith is carrying a file folder that is so full it is bursting at its seams. Written upon it is NEO's name and it apparently contains NEO's life's history. Naturally, NEO is intensely curious about the folder but he isn't given an opportunity to examine it. I'd often walk into an interrogation room carrying just such a folder, but in my case, it normally contained 99% trash. But Pinocchio doesn't know that! He'll think it contains overwhelming evidence of his guilt.

There is no such thing as FLURB, by the way … But how much did you buy into the concept? The point I'm making is that you can make up your own "evidence" and Pinocchio will be none the wiser. Pinocchio will be so focused upon trying to escape the net you're weaving that he doesn't have time to consider whether FLURB or any other evidence really exists. Perhaps you don't think anyone would **really** fall for something like FLURB, but you'd be **very** wrong. I've used FLURB on hardened convicts who've been through the system so many times that most cops would think nobody could get them to confess. In fact, I've even used it on cops without them detecting the deceit! After all, do you really understand how your microwave oven or television works? Crime shows like CSI and others have taught the public that almost anything is possible with today's forensic technology.

Some of you, no doubt, will regard the prospect of lying to suspected liars distasteful. There are certainly moral—and sometimes legal—issues with which one must contend when using deception to get a confession. I've had students in my classes voice the same concerns, but these are the reasons lying is allowed by law enforcement officers in their dealings with the public:

• The Supreme Court has ruled that without the use of deception, police are unlikely to get a confession in most cases. After all, unless Pinocchio thinks you know the truth, why confess?

• The use of deception is fine so long as it doesn't "shock the consciousness of the community." In other words, a cop can't pretend to be a priest or a lawyer, thereby tricking Pinocchio into thinking he's speaking with someone who cannot use his words against him. Nor can cops create such convincing evidence that it would force an otherwise innocent person to confess (such as using Photoshop to put Pinocchio into a crime scene video).

• Deception should be used sparingly on those with emotional and mental deficits because it can cause a person with those handicaps to falsely confess when they are innocent.

While you may have reservations about lying to Pinocchio, you must realize that the Supreme Court wrestled with those same reservations and decided in the end that there is often no way to avoid lying **if you want the truth**. That, my friends, is the crux of the matter if you don't have any real evidence. While I wish the world were different, as Dr. Phil so often says, "It is what it is."

STEP SIX: CONFRONTATION

So you've decided what you'll use as your "evidence"—be it real or fabricated—and you're ready to use it. But what you need to learn is **how** to use it.

The confrontation serves two purposes:

• The first is to confirm that Pinocchio is lying. Remember, truthful people tend to speak and act in certain ways, just as liars tend to speak and act in other ways. When you confront Pinocchio, you're watching for more indicators of deception. A truthful person will probably make a forceful denial to your accusation; a deceptive person, though, will likely exhibit more deceptive behaviors and make—at best—a weak denial.

- The second purpose is to convince Pinocchio you have evidence of his guilt and that the game is over. All that he needs to do now is to decide how to package and deliver his confession.

Many people are uncertain about when or to confront Pinocchio. After all, it isn't always necessary to get a confession that he's lying or has lied to you. Let's say that you've decided a car salesman is lying about a particular car—be it about the available rebates, its mechanical and maintenance history or anything else. In a situation like that, it's probably just better to walk away and find a more honest salesman.

How you confront Pinocchio is extremely important. You must do so in a confident manner and in a way that projects earnestness. You cannot come across as judgmental or act as if you're selling a product; rather, this is Pinocchio's chance to resolve an issue troubling **both** of you.

What I've always done, if possible, is ensure that I'm standing and Pinocchio is sitting, assumed a dominant stance (my legs spread shoulder-width apart and arms open with the palms facing up), and said, "Pinocchio, I know you weren't entirely truthful about this matter. **We need to talk about this issue.**" (Note this use of the term "we." You're implying you're both in this together!)

This is Pinocchio's last chance to make a firm denial. Honest people will usually make a firm denial at this point and protest their innocence. Pinocchio may make a weak attempt at denial, but often, he'll say nothing or look away from you. Even better, he may go immediately into what Stan Walters calls the "surrender position." This is when Pinocchio almost literally melts into his chair and is poised with his head, neck and trunk bowed forward with his arms lying loosely upon his legs or out to his sides.

Let's assume, though, that Pinocchio doesn't go immediately into the surrender position. What you must do now is think back to what Pinocchio said in response to your questions—these will assist you in your next step: giving Pinocchio an excuse for what he did!

STEP SEVEN: OVERCOMING BARRIERS, OBJECTIONS AND OBSTACLES

If Pinocchio tries to interrupt you when you are confronting him, realize this is a stalling tactic and don't fall for it. He may say something like, "I couldn't kill her, I don't even own a gun." If you analyze that statement, you'll see that Pinocchio doesn't deny killing our fictitious lady, he just denies owning a gun … (I know of several murder cases in which suspects have said just the same thing.)

To stop Pinocchio from using these stalling tactics, raise your hand in front of you like a cop stops traffic, and say, "Pinocchio, we'll talk about that in a moment, but right now, I want you to listen to me." You can even turn these weak denials against him. For example, with the above stalling tactic, you could say, "Pinocchio, I'm glad you said that because it tells me you aren't a violent man. If you owned a gun, that would mean you're predisposed to committing this type of thing. This had to be a spur of the moment thing, something caused by extreme stress. You wouldn't do this normally."

Remember that liars will make weak or no denials, but truthful people will make strong denials that usually will not falter throughout your confrontation. If Pinocchio makes a strong denial and those denials continue to strengthen, then you need to re-evaluate your assessment of Pinocchio's honesty. But if Pinocchio's denials are nonexistent, weak and getting weaker, it's time to move onto the next step.

STEP EIGHT: THEME DEVELOPMENT

During theme development, you are creating a storyline for Pinocchio to buy into. The theme you use is nothing more than a rationalization for Pinocchio's actions. The rationalization itself doesn't matter; the thing that does matter is that Pinocchio buys into and uses it as his justification for doing whatever wrong he committed. It need not have any semblance to reality, and Pinocchio need not believe in it; he must, though, assume that you believe it.

If you had the opportunity to ask Pinocchio those questions we discussed earlier, then you'll probably have ample material from which to create a theme. But even if you couldn't ask any or many of those questions, you can still come up with themes to use. Here are some commonly used themes that have stood the test of time. Let's take cheating, for example:

1. Blame the victim: (You yourself can be that victim.) It's not Pinocchio's fault that he cheated on you. You've both drifted apart over time, and naturally, he got lonely and needed to someone to whom he could talk.

2. Blame stress: Certainly, things have been rough for him at work. You know he wouldn't normally act this way, and he just happened to make a bad deci-

sion. It was a one-time moment of weakness and you just need to know it'll never happen again.

3.   Blame a friend: It would have happened if he hadn't been with Evil Ed. Evil Ed has caused other men to do bad things and has a wild side. If EE hadn't caused Pinocchio to drink so much and go to that bar, then none of this would have happened!

Themes can be combined too, in order to give Pinocchio a wide variety of excuses for his behavior. What you are seeking is a combination or central theme that Pinocchio likes. You'll be able to tell when your theme has struck a chord with Pinocchio because he'll often show heightened interest in what you're saying by leaning forward, licking his lips and other signs of heightened interest in your words. He may even nod and visibly relax.

I once worked for a company as a sales director, and in a closed door meeting, the VP of Sales asked me about a facsimile I'd sent to one of our clients. She said, "I **think** I found it by the fax machine." She said it wasn't a big deal, but all the while she was kicking the air with her left leg. This let me know two things: She didn't find it at the fax machine, for one, and for two, it was a big deal. Apparently, I'd violated a company rule of which I wasn't familiar. But moreover, someone had taken the trouble to take that fax to the VP in order to cause me misery rather than speak with me one-on-one.

I thanked the VP for her feedback, apologized for the error, and said, "I know you have a hard job babysitting all the different personalities around here and would rather not deal with these issues yourself. If you'll tell me who brought this error to your attention, I'd like to thank her and apologize in person. I appreciate her assistance in helping me better understand the company's rules regarding this type of information."

The VP thought this was a grand idea, and told me the person's name—apparently never realizing that I'd caught her in a lie and gotten a confession. And from then on, I knew there was a certain co-worker whom I could never trust!

Sometimes, you have to try several themes before you find the exact combination or single theme that works. In one interview with a man we'll call Doug, I tried every trick I could think of when trying to get Doug to confess to stealing a fellow employee's car stereo. I was able to establish rapport with him early on, and I implied that I had video footage of him breaking into the car and taking the stereo, but he wasn't buying any theme I tried. At the end of four hours of talking, I was worn out and ready to call it quits. Just as I was getting ready to end the interview and try again another day, Doug turned to me, his hand on the door knob of my cubicle, and said, "Do you believe in God?"

I hadn't tried religion as a theme because I had no indication Doug was religious. Apparently, in the months following the burglary, he had converted to Christianity and no one I spoke with knew of this event. Doug stepped back into my office and we talked for another hour, during which time he gave a full confession. Not only that, he told me that he'd had a moment of epiphany about how theft affects one personally, because someone had recently broken into his truck and stolen "his" stereo. It turned out Doug's stereo was the one he'd stolen from the co-worker, and Doug was outraged that someone would dare steal it from him!

STEP NINE: PERSUASION TECHNIQUES

While you are using your theme upon Pinocchio, you might consider using some tried and true persuasion techniques. Many of these techniques came originally from the sales and advertising industry, and all have been proven in scientific studies to be highly effective in persuading others to do as you want.

These persuasion techniques can be incorporated into your strategy at any point in the interview, but it's best to use them sparingly. I myself usually never use more than three in one interview; if you use more than three of these techniques, you run the risk that Pinocchio will recognize you are running a game on him. Let's discuss the most effective techniques:

- **Authority & Power**: Our society is built around a hierarchical structure. While we may all have the same basic human right afforded to us, that doesn't mean that some people do not command more power and respect than others. Since humans are social animals, we tend to look to those in authority and to our more "important" peers whenever we are under lots of stress. If you project power and confidence via your clothing and body language, you are much more likely to obtain a confession than if you are shabbily dressed and act less than confident. For those of you who conduct investigations, the traditional dark power suit is a must-have item for your wardrobe. But even when performing such mundane tasks as buying a car, I'll wear my most impressive suit and watch because these items are an excellent psychological edge. I've gone to different car dealerships in the past and consistently wrangled better deals on the same vehicle on the same day just because I wore a suit. I've also noticed salespeople are also more honest with me when I'm wearing a high status clothing and jewelry.

- **Reciprocity**: This is one of the most easily used of the techniques. In fact, it's probably been used on you quite often! Any time you receive a "free gift with purchase" at a department store, a sheaf of address stickers in the mail from a charity, or a soft drink from a car salesperson, reciprocity is being used upon you. The "hook" here is that if someone gives you something, you're beholden to that person. Research has shown that you're much more likely to comply with any request that person makes of you. Salespeople sell more merchandise (cars, perfume, etc.) whenever they give (or promise to) you something. Every time Pinocchio walked into my office, I'd buy him his drink of choice before we started talking.

- **Scarcity**: At one time, diamonds were scarce commodities and were extremely difficult to find. Today, though, one can walk into any large mall and see more diamonds on display than many nations possessed not so long ago. Why then do we pay so much for them? While our culture has taught us that diamonds are scarce, they are not. In reality, the diamond trade is closely regulated by the owners of the world's largest diamond mines. Those mine owners are very careful to not allow the market to be "flooded" with their products. If they allowed too many diamonds onto the market, the value of diamonds would drop dramatically. We see this technique used in many tourist sectors of the world as well. For example, I live in Orlando, Florida, and there are many stores that have had "going out of business" banners in their windows for years now. Going out of business has become an extremely profitable business strategy here in Florida. Tourists visiting and locals who live in Orlando all fall for this tactic time and again. When Pinocchio is involved with a group that has done something wrong, you would suggest that his options for confessing are limited. He who tells the truth first reaps the benefits of doing so; the others have missed their opportunity once one member confesses.

- **Liking & Similarity**: As I stated in an earlier chapter, the more similar Pinocchio perceives you to be to him and the more he likes you, the easier it is to get him to confess to you. In this game, just like in sales, the most important thing is getting that first "Yes." After that, everything becomes much easier. By establishing some common ground between you and Pinocchio, you'll make it much harder for him to resist your overtures. The more he likes you, the much more likely he is to confess to you.

- **Commitment & Consistency**: This builds onto my last statement about getting that first "Yes" out of Pinocchio. If you can get him to talk to you about one subject—be it fishing, dancing or whatever—he will be extremely likely to continue talking to you about the subject in which you are **truly** interested. There have been numerous studies that have proven this principle's effectiveness time and again. In the so-called real world, non-profit companies and charities realize that if you contribute to their causes one time, you will usually continue to contribute for years to come. This is because part of our biological programming tells us to continue doing what has worked for us in the past; also, our society and culture depends on its people acting in somewhat predictable fashions. From birth, we've been taught that nonconformity results in sanctions against us—it is society's way of reigning us in—and we internalize those lessons by suppressing any wayward impulses we might feel toward society's restrictions on our behavior (we'll talk about the power of authority figures soon too). There are a few ways you can use this programming against Pinocchio:

1. **Get Pinocchio talking and keep him talking**. The more he talks, the more chances you have to not only judge his honesty, but getting him to talk about his offense becomes much easier.

2. **Get an admission to a small offense first.** To illustrate how effective this principle can be, one study had students go door-to-door and ask homeowners if they'd allow the students to put a small political sign in their front yards. Those homeowners (about 75%) who agreed had the sign planted in their front yards. Those same homeowners were revisited a few months later. This time, those students asked the homeowners if they'd agree to let the students place signs in their front yards that were so large that they would block the view of the homes from the street. Better than 33% of those homeowners agreed to the new signs (which weren't really put on their properties).

3. **Accuse Pinocchio of doing something much worse than you suspect he committed**. Pinocchio will often deny the larger offense but admit the smaller (true) offense. There are a couple of reasons for this behavior. Pinocchio doesn't want to be blamed for something he did not do, and one way to prove his innocence to the larger offense is to confess to the smaller one. By confessing to the smaller offense, he de facto proves his innocence to the larger. Psychologically, it's much easier for Pinocchio to confess to a smaller offense than the larger. In a mirror study to the one involving students and political signs, those same students went to a different neighborhood and asked homeowners if they would agree to place the large sign in their front yards. Almost all—97%—declined to have the

large sign placed in their front yards (can you blame them?). However, the students—immediately after getting the refusal—then asked if they could place the small sign in the homeowners' front yards. While we might expect a second refusal, the homeowners' agreed better than 77% of the time to allow the students to put the small sign in their front yards. But why? Social scientists theorize that our culture makes it harder for us to say no to people; therefore, while we can easily ignore a "large" request, a smaller and hypothetically smaller request triggers our societal programming to cooperate with others—so we agree to the smaller request.

4. **A full confession may bear more fruit.** Once you've resolved the matter at hand, ask if anything else Pinocchio might have done. Doctors, in particular, are familiar with patients who will say nothing else is wrong with them during a physical examination, but at the last second (with a little prodding) will mention an aggravating mole that turns out to be cancerous (or other hidden condition) missed by the doctor. It's sometimes referred to as the, "By The Way Syndrome." Something I always do is say, "Look, I know there's something else you haven't told me." Then, I just stare at Pinocchio and let him speak first. Sometimes, Pinocchio will volunteer information about things with which you never suspected he had any connection.

STEP TEN: RECOGNIZING WHEN YOUR TECHNIQUES ARE WORKING

Some people are very emotional and when you find the theme they like, they will become tearful and very remorseful in appearance. Others are non-emotional, and they will likely show much fewer signs of surrender. What you must look for is evidence of relaxation and interest in your theme. The classic surrender position is the one we discussed before: head bowed, body leaning forward and arms hanging loosely.

Another behavior Pinocchio may exhibit is what my friend Stan Walters calls "bargaining." Bargaining is when Pinocchio asks questions like "What will happen to me if I did this?" or says, "It'll never happen again." Tactics like this are Pinocchio's method of implicitly asking for forgiveness while not explicitly confessing to the offense; he's "testing the waters" and trying to decide whether he should confess or not. You shouldn't tell Pinocchio what will happen to him if he confesses. Your best response to Pinocchio's bargaining gambit is to say, "Would you rather deal with someone who's admitted he made a mistake or someone who continues to lie even after the truth is known?"

You'll find that once Pinocchio begins to demonstrate bargaining behaviors, he's almost ready to move into the surrender phase. It may take time to get to the surrender stage, but something to remember is that even though liars will deny they are being deceptive, those denials will become weaker over time. An honest person's denials become stronger (and often more strident). Your job isn't to brow-beat Pinocchio, though; what you must do is act in a level-headed and calm manner. If you threaten or bully Pinocchio, you run the risk of getting a false confession.

Given enough time and the proper pressure, nearly anyone can be broken and will give a false confession. Just ask anyone who has spent time in the Hanoi Hilton during the Vietnam War or any other prisoner of war camp. If you notice that Pinocchio's denials consistently get stronger, it's time to back off and reconsider your opinion of his honesty. If, however, you see Pinocchio begin to evaluate your theme and then later go into surrender mode, it's time to move to the next stage!

STEP ELEVEN: THE DIVERGENT QUESTION TECHNIQUE

Different interviewing schools identify this technique by numerous names, but I prefer the term divergent because it gives Pinocchio two paths to go down. One path leads to the truth—our preferred path—while on the other path, Pinocchio continues his deception. Our job is to make the pathway to honesty the more palatable of his two choices. It's at this point—when Pinocchio is at the surrender stage and weakest psychologically—that we want to give him a method of releasing all his stress. If you recall when we discussed the so-called "trauma of deceit" and the physiological stressors lying can inflict upon the body, you'll realize that Pinocchio will be seeking a way to alleviate his stress.

Obtaining a confession can be expressed as a simple algebraic equation: $C = T(P+U)$. For those of you who haven't guessed, this means a Confession equals Time multiplied by (Pressure plus Uncertainty). What the Divergent Question does—if asked at the proper Time when Pinocchio is most Uncertain—is apply psychological Pressure that will lead to Pinocchio giving you a Confession.

What the divergent question does is offer Pinocchio two choices:

1.   Continue to lie and experience the associated stressors of deception.

2.   Confess and alleviate that stress.

The first thing to do is to set the stage for Pinocchio by **increasing** his stress. Start by telling Pinocchio, "Look, Pinocchio, I know you did this thing, and I know you're not a bad guy. But we need to sort this out."

What you are doing is letting him know that although you understand how difficult the situation is for him, the stress isn't going to stop until **you** are satisfied with **his** answers. Next, you'll be offering Pinocchio a glimpse of the light at the end of this tunnel in which he's found himself by offering him those two choices we discussed earlier.

The divergent question makes Pinocchio choose between "good" reasons for what he did versus "bad" reasons. Many people get hung up on what two questions to ask Pinocchio when, in reality, the questions themselves means little beyond their psychological influence upon Pinocchio. All you need to do is incorporate the theme you've already been using and roll it into a question; after that, think of a question that incorporate its polar opposite.

Let's say you believe Pinocchio, a former alcoholic, has begun drinking again. In your theme, you probably would emphasize the stress in Pinocchio's life, which caused him to pick up the bottle again.

What we would do is compress our theme by saying, "Pinocchio, I know the stress has been hard on you, and stress can make us do things we don't want to do so we can cope with it. Pinocchio, I've got to know, are you drinking again because of the stress or are you doing it because you just don't care about us? I believe the stress just got to you. That's it, isn't it?"

I've heard a lot of criticism over the years about this technique from people who think it's a form of entrapment and unethical. I've used it time and again to get hardened criminals to sell me years of their lives (years that, in many cases, were spent in State of Florida and federal prisons) and it's so effective that defense lawyers and legal scholars throw fits when it's been used in high profile cases. What most fail to understand (and the rest ignore) is that innocent people—barring undue pressure—won't fall for the divergent question, but the guilty, who are grasping at straws, will seize upon it. Like any tool, the divergent question technique can be and has been abused. Unfortunately, the abuses get far more publicity than the proper uses of the technique.

If Pinocchio rejects the divergent question, you have to decide whether you were wrong about his honesty. If Pinocchio exhibited deceptive behavior(s), engaged in bargaining, and showed surrender to your theme, then he's likely having "buyer's remorse" and merely needs more time before he'll confess.

Sometimes, you'll get interrupted during the divergent question (or any other) stage, which may cause Pinocchio to back-track. In that case, you'll need to restate your theme and start over; sometimes, you will need to use an entirely different theme and divergent question. Because interruptions can be so detrimental to the process, I always recommend you turn off all phones and remove any distractions. Personally, I don't even wear a watch when talking with Pinocchio. I've seen perfectly executed interviews derailed because someone glanced at his watch and nonverbally reminded Pinocchio how long they've been talking. Not only does it remind Pinocchio of where he is and what he's doing, but it also implies to him that if he can wait a little longer, you'll be the first one to surrender.

If Pinocchio begins exhibiting behavior such as nodding or moves into the surrender position, you can be reasonably certain that he's ready for the divergent question. Now is the time to move in for the kill.

Again, all you must do is give Pinocchio a choice between a good reason versus a bad one for doing what he did. Remember, even Hitler thought he was justified in his actions. Nor are you pushing for a complete confession at this juncture. All you want is for Pinocchio to either say, "Yes" or to totally repeat the "good" reason.

Just like in a sales meeting, all we're seeking is the buy-in. Once Pinocchio commits to the divergent question, now you can get the full confession. First, start by thanking Pinocchio for opening up to you. Then, tell Pinocchio you need to know exactly what happened.

Once you get all the details, go over them again and be alert for further deception. Be conscious of the fact that Pinocchio may not tell you all the truth at first and may need additional prompting. The longer he talks, the better your chances become for extracting **all** the truth from him. Something I personally do each time Pinocchio confesses to me is say, "There's something else you want to tell me, isn't there, Pinocchio?"

You might be surprised at what else Pinocchio tells you.

As I always tell my students, once Pinocchio finally comes clean and confesses, thank him for his honesty. You'll never know when he'll be a repeat customer!

In the next chapter, we'll discuss the most feared machine next to the electric chair: the lie detector!

Things to Remember

- Talk alone. Pinocchio will want privacy when he confesses. Don't confront him in public or in the presence of another person. The pressure to continue lying will be too great if you don't adhere to this principle.

- Small talk first. Don't rush into things.

- Use the S.O.F.T.E.N. Technique to increase Pinocchio's feeling of closeness to you.

- Projecting confidence and implying you already know the truth is crucial to your success.

- Use the appropriate persuasion technique and know what you want to get from Pinocchio. Do you want a full confession to a specific act or just an admission that he lied?

- Think of the interrogation like a debate and attempt to anticipate what Pinocchio will say or do in his defense. That way, you can be at least one step ahead of him.

7

Polygraphs & Other Lie Detectors

The polygraph—don't make it move
One little twitch, the anvil drops on you

—Dead Kennedys, *Lie Detector*

Man has long sought a reliable method of determining if his fellow humans are lying to him. The ancient Hindus made suspected liars chew dry rice in the belief that once spat out a liar's mouthful of rice would remain dry while a truthful person's mouthful of rice would become moist due to saliva saturating it. Physiologically, the approach was quite insightful. We now know that there are many physiological markers of the stress deception can produce in our bodies (I've referred to this phenomenon before in this book as the "trauma of deceit").

THE POLYGRAPH

The first version of the device we call the "lie detector" or the polygraph was invented by James Mackenzie in 1902. However, that machine was a failure, and the modern polygraph owes its roots to a medical student named John Larson, who invented it in 1921.

People erroneously believe the polygraph and other so-called lie detectors can determine if someone is lying. What the best of these devices actually measure is the stress lying causes someone; some of these machines, however, can't even measure that.

The most commonly configured polygraph measures a person's chest expansion (for respiration), pulse rate, blood pressure, and perspiration via galvanic skin response (the two clips attached to the fingers). Significant changes in these bodily responses indicate a stress reaction and are believed to be indicators of deception. In order to properly measure deviations to the person's normal biological state, though, the polygraph examiner must first obtain a baseline measurement of the person's stress-free reactions. Once the examiner is confident he has a good baseline measurement, then he asks the person a series of questions—some meaningful, others not.

Throughout the test, the polygraph examiner monitors the subject's autonomic responses and decides if there are any areas upon which he should focus his attention. Let's say that you have normal responses to all the questions except to those questions concerning marijuana use. The examiner would then ask you more questions about drug use.

The problem with the polygraph is that its examiners tend to place an overwhelming belief in its capabilities. Along with this belief comes a great propensity for misjudging someone's innocence. Let's say you had a cousin who died of a drug overdose. Might not the topic of drugs or drug use make you stressed?

The polygraph is specifically designed to induce and measure stress, but so many things can induce stress because our minds cannot separate perceived stress versus real stress. Take roller coasters, for example: What makes one person love them but horrify another person? Surely the physical experience—the G-forces, centrifugal turns, and loops, etc.—is the same for both people! But for one person, the metabolic and physiological responses will be off the chart, while the other person may only experience a heightened pulse rate.

But it gets even stranger. When the person who is terrified of roller coasters thinks of riding one—just thinks about it—that person very well may exhibit the same physiological responses as when he is riding a roller coaster! So if a polygraph examiner asked you about stealing, and you happen to recall when someone stole your car stereo, you may feel rage. The polygraph cannot tell which emotion you are feeling; it only knows you are in a state of heightened arousal. That arousal will register as deception, and although polygraph examiners are supposed to explore what is causing the arousal, my experience has been that most examiners will simply label you a liar.

Polygraph effectiveness is alleged by its proponents to be somewhere around 80% to 90%. But just like cops who deal with a subset of the population who are guilty of something, polygraph examiners often develop an over-inflated sense of their effectiveness as lie-catchers. Also, if all you're doing is saying someone passes or fails, there are few—if any—controls in place that makes certain you are correct in your assessment. Many people have lost job opportunities in the federal government and law enforcement because they failed their polygraph screenings. In fact, in 1998, Congress passed the Employee Polygraph Protection Act (Title 29 United States Code Chapter 22) that prohibits most employers from giving polygraphs to their employees. After the Act was passed, many polygraph operators closed up their shops. Only employees or potential employees involved in national security or law enforcement work can be forced to undergo a polygraph exam as a condition of their employment.

If polygraphs were truly effective "lie detectors," one would think their use would be allowed as evidence in court, but in most circumstances, they are not. This is because the polygraph does not meet the Supreme Court's definition of a scientific instrument as held under the Daubert v. Merrell Dow Pharmaceuticals, Inc., 113 S. Ct. 2786 (1993) ruling. To date, the only time a polygraph test is admissible is if both plaintiff and defense counsel agree to the test's inclusion. This applies to criminal trials (in which the standard of proof is beyond a reasonable doubt) and civil trials (with the much lower standard of a simple preponderance of evidence).

THE POLYGRAPH'S FLAWS

As we've learned, the polygraph operates by monitoring a person's biological state, and there are those people who don't react or show very little reaction when lying. We usually term such people sociopaths. Of course, people who are under the influence of psychotropic drugs or other mood-altering chemicals are also difficult for a polygraph to read. The same is true for giving a polygraph exam to a mentally ill person; once someone's baseline biological responses are altered or unreadable, the polygraph is of little use.

The polygraph is also easily defeated by those who have uncommon control over their bodies. Anyone who has had biofeedback training can easily circumvent a polygraph. But even if you aren't a yoga master or haven't had advanced training in controlling your body's metabolism, you too can defeat a polygraph. The polygraph examiner's first task is to get a baseline of your body's normal responses, and if he cannot do that, his machine is useless. One way of keeping him from getting that baseline is when he asks a "normal" question is to tighten your anal sphincter muscle. This simple act causes an increase in blood pressure, pulse rate, and galvanic skin response. When you are asked a "targeted" question—such as if you've ever stolen anything—all you need to do is relax. This stops the examiner from getting the baseline and results in an inconclusive test. There are several techniques used by polygraph examiners to determine if a person is being dishonest or has "guilty knowledge" of a crime (or other wrongdoing). For example, you could be shown pictures of several people or items. Some (or one) of those people and/or items would be associated with the matter under investigation. If your body shows a spike in its physiological responses when you are asked or shown a picture of significance, you are judged to have knowledge of the matter.

Another problem with the polygraph is that some people simply cannot pass them due to being too excitable in general or too worried about the investigation in specific. I've known people to take polygraphs and fail them on one day and pass them on the next day.

Polygraph examiners themselves are another issue altogether. I've seen two polygraph examiners review the same test and reach extremely different conclusions about the person's honesty. And much of the polygraph test's outcome also depends upon how the examiner treats the person he is testing. I've personally witnessed examiners who were so abrasive and openly antagonistic when conducting their exams that it's a wonder anyone was able to pass their tests. Contrast that with other examiners who are professional and solicitous in their demeanor, and you can imagine how these two different types of examiners could elicit different results from their subjects.

While the polygraph is the most well-known lie detector, there are many others on the market, and most are available for purchase by the general public.

THE COMPUTERIZED VOICE STRESS ANALYZER (CVSA)™

The CVSA™ has gained in popularity in recent years and has been used by numerous local, state, and federal agencies. It has even purportedly been used by civilian contractors in Iraq to determine whether suspected terrorists should be granted freedom.

The CVSA, unlike the polygraph, has absolutely no known scientific basis. But despite this fact, the CVSA allegedly is in use by over 1500 federal, state, county and city law enforcement agencies in criminal investigations.

The CVSA purportedly detects deception by analyzing micro-tremors in a deceptive person's voice. Honest people are not supposed to exhibit these "micro-tremors" or do so in an altered form. The problem with this premise is that there has never been a significant scientific study that supports the CVSA's ability to detect deception; there have been, however, numerous studies that show ability of a trained CVSA operator to detect deception is no better than chance. While the polygraph has at least the benefit of being able to measure demonstrable bodily functions, there is no evidence that the CVSA's "micro-tremors" even exist.

The National Institute for Truth Verification, the company that produces the CVSA and trains people how to use its product, states that its success is not measured by scientific studies, but by how many confessions its technology has obtained and the number of law enforcement agencies using its technology. As we've discussed, though, much of what causes a guilty person to confess is the **belief** that the interrogator already knows he is lying. Unfortunately, the false belief of a CVSA operator that someone is lying can not only lead to innocent people being accused of committing crimes, but also increases the risk of false confessions. While a number of law enforcement agencies have stopped using the CVSA because of its bad press, there are many more waiting in the wings to take their places.

FUNCTIONAL MAGNETIC RESONANCE IMAGING

The most exciting development in lie detection is the Functional MRI. This device is able to show blood flowing throughout the brain, and more importantly, increases in that blood flow. Since the brain uses only glucose as fuel, an increase in blood flow to the one portion of the brain indicates an increased need for glucose. In essence, the F-MRI shows the brain at work.

Liars would be expected to show increased blood flow to the brain's frontal lobes—the "thinking portion" of the brain—and truth-tellers would be expected to show more blood flow to their memory centers.

In controlled studies, F-MRI scans have consistently been able to identify 100% of truth-tellers and it can detect liars 90% of the time. In other words, the F-MRI is a tool that can almost conclusively prove innocence of those people accused of wrong-doing, and it very well may be accepted by the Court as a scientific instrument for proving truthfulness.

As this technology is perfected, I expect it to be used not to convict people of crimes, but rather, to prove people are innocent of them. There are some companies that are now gearing up to bring this technology to the marketplace, and I expect that in the near future, attorneys will be attempting to introduce F-MRI scans as proof of their clients' innocence.

OTHER LIE DETECTION PRODUCTS

There are a number of devices that purport to detect lies being sold and even made today. For example, one individual even created a lie detector out of a Lego's™ electronics kit (see http://www.engadget.com/2006/03/24/lego-lie-detector-makes-interrogations-fun/) that measures galvanic skin response! While that device is a simple one, it's probably more effective than many others out there.

Even phone companies like Skype ™ are getting in on the action. Skype is to offer its customers the opportunity to purchase the KishKish Lie Detector™ in 2008. This device purports to measure stress levels of people by examining radio waves. As yet, Skype has not released prices (or any research data!) for customers. And the Department of Defense has been soliciting bids for companies to create a device that will measure heart, pulse and respiration rates via laser beams. This device will enable soldiers and government agents to covertly determine if an individual is experiencing physiological stress without the need to hook him up to a machine.

Most lie detection devices sold to the civilian market are unproven gimmicks that do nothing more than detect the fact that you have money to waste. They may be fun to use at parties, but that's the extent of their usefulness. That, however, may soon change.

Companies like Emotiv Systems, Inc. are putting the finishing touches on headsets that will be able to read emotions via brainwaves and allow game players to control avatars in the online world. If these devices truly work as promised, it won't be long before they are adapted to work in the real world. In fact, an article in PC Magazine hints that the law enforcement and national security communities are already interested in exploring the capability of this technology.

THE BELIEF FACTOR

The most potent factor any type of "lie detector" has in its favor is that people fear and believe in them. Most people are under the mistaken impression that the polygraph somehow discerns truth versus falsehood; we know, though, that effective lie detectors actually detect physiological stress, not deception.

Like voodoo, if you believe in it, the polygraph and its operator gain more control over you. It then becomes a weapon of intimidation and psychological coercion. To give you an idea about how powerful the suggestion one has failed a polygraph can be, let me tell you the story about a burglar we'll call "Joey."

We knew Joey had broken into a store, but Joey was a hard-core, stone cold criminal. He'd been interviewed numerous times before and he knew we didn't have any evidence on him. When the lead detective grew weary of playing with Joey, he asked Joey if he'd be willing to take a polygraph test. I was a rookie patrolman at the time, and although I knew very little about how our detectives worked at that time, I did know one thing: **My department didn't have a polygraph.**

I was stunned when the detective walked Joey over to the copier machine, reached down and grabbed what appeared to be a metal colander with wires attached to it that appeared to be connected to the copier machine. Joey was told to sit down in the closest chair, and the detective placed the colander on Joey's head.

The detective asked Joey only one thing and one thing only: "Joey, you broke into that store, didn't you?" When Joey laughed and said, "No," the detective pushed the copy button and out rolled a piece of paper that had "LIAR" printed upon it in large, bold type.

The detective held up that piece of paper in front of Joey and said nothing at all. For what seemed like an eternity—but was probably only a minute or two—the detective silently stood there. Finally, Joey leaned forward and put his head in his hands, and confessed to not one, but seven burglaries. I, though, had to leave the room because I thought I was going to burst into laughter.

Later, I asked the detective about his "polygraph" test. He said the detectives always kept a sheet of paper that said "**LIAR**" in the copier machine for just such occasions. Often, he said, they wound up ruining the first page of whenever they were copying something because they usually forgot to take out their fake test result paper.

The point I'm making is that even if the device you use is a box of useless lights and wires—or a Lego's toy—it is often Pinocchio's belief in its effectiveness that determines effectiveness. Conversely, the less Pinocchio believes in the device and the less stress it causes him, the less likely you are to obtain a confession with it.

Things to Remember

- Polygraphs and other current "lie detectors" do not detect lies—they detect physiological responses to the stress caused by deception.

- The more Pinocchio believes in the lie detector device, the more susceptible he is to it.

- The F-MRI may be the only exception that the above points. It may prove to be able to show the brain's "deception mechanism." However, studies are not yet complete on this promising technology, and the F-MRI machines are going to be expensive.

- Polygraphs and other lie detectors are not considered to be scientific instruments by the court, and their results are inadmissible as evidence unless both sides' attorneys agree to its inclusion (and the presiding judge agrees).

8

The Games People Play (With You)

If I'm telling you the truth right now, do you believe it
Games people play in the middle of the night

— The Alan Parsons Project, *Games People Play*

One of the first principles I introduced to you is that people miss 50% or more of the blackest lies told to them. Those are the big lies, the ones that have the most potential to cause you harm. However, by now you must realize there are far many more lies told to you all the time. How many lies are told to you, though, is largely a matter of definition. And that definition is very loose indeed.

And if you recall my segment on meta-communication, then you know that communication consists of not just the words themselves, but also of the underlying feelings of the communicator. Interpersonal communication itself, though, has many dynamics surrounding it. It's not just how the communicator feels about you, but also about herself, the surrounding social situation, and the topic itself.

Some social scientists have gone so far as to propose that we are never truly the same person in different social situations. For example, when with my best friend David, with whom I've been friends since I was eleven years old, I'm entirely comfortable cracking jokes and acting like we're still in high school. We have a language of sorts that consists of stories about past experiences, jokes, and quirks that other people—including our wives—simply don't understand.

David's wife still tells a story about the time she watched us working on a well together.: David—who actually knew what he was doing—was bent into an awkward position working on it and would look up, and I'd hand him a specific tool. This would occur without either of us saying a word to the other. When Tammy asked how I knew which tool to hand David without him asking for it or being

111

able to see what he was doing, I couldn't tell her. We'd worked on our beat-up cars together since we both were 15 years old, and I was accustomed to his body language.

With my supervisors at work, though, I'm much more reserved, but even then, I feel differently and act differently with each one of them. And when I'm teaching a class or conducting a seminar, I feel and act differently when addressing the group than the individuals one-on-one. I enjoy public speaking, but I'm slow to warm up to individuals.

While you may intuitively realize this to be true for yourself as well, what you may not know is that it's true for everyone. You probably don't realize it in others, however, because when you interact with Joey at the office, you're seeing that aspect of Joey that feeds off your personality. Joey is an entirely different person with his wife Cindy, and likewise, with your mutual boss at work. The person you know as Joey may very well walk, talk, and act quite differently than when he is with you.

Regardless of which aspect of his personality Joey is presenting to whomever he is communicating, there is generally one constant to his communication: Joey will try to portray himself in the most favorable light possible.

Herein lies the problem with all human communication: it is almost always contains some alteration, some "spin" on it that favors the communicator. One of more well-known personalities in my line of business, Avinoam Sapir, states 90% of the lies we tell contain some element of truth. He believes—and I agree—most people hedge, omit crucial facts, feign forgetfulness, and pretend ignorance rather than tell complete falsehoods. I also believe, though, that the inverse is true as well, and that 90% of the truth contains some degree of falsehood, "spin," or perhaps just the slanting of the communicator's unique perspective. Consider the common commercial: The product it advertises may do everything it claims, but perhaps not with the ease or the speed it implies. Drugs—particularly the over the counter ones in my experience—are notorious in this fashion. Tonight, I went to my local pharmacy (and a company in which I own stock) for something to ease a particularly nasty cough I'd developed. When looking at the labels and the symptoms they promised to treat, I was overwhelmed by the sheer number of choices one brand offered. Did I want something that inhibited the cough or make the cough more productive? I also could choose a combination that would reduce fever and help me sleep. Finally, I resorted to reading the ingredients; much to my surprise, almost all of the combinations—I believe there were four or five—had the exact same ingredients! The

"Cold & Flu" version of the cough syrup was the same formulation as the regular cough syrup.

The makers of Head On™—yes, the creators of that amazingly annoying commercial!—were sued by the FDA because there was no proof their product actually prevents or cures headaches. Instead of pulling the product from stores, the manufacturers removed the claims and simply kept the rest of the annoying commercial. And guess what? Sales actually increased dramatically! (So much so that they now have a new product that doesn't claim to do anything either!)

The problem with trying to undercover every single piece of deception in your life is that you run the risk of driving yourself crazy (or of becoming very paranoid, anyway!). A friend of mine, Bonnie, told me the first time we met that she'd be terrified of being married to someone like me because she felt she'd always be scrutinized.

What Bonnie didn't realize is that I don't have the time, inclination, or ability to examine every single conversation, e-mail or television commercial for deception. I've come to understand that people and organizations all want to accomplish something when they communicate with me, and that they will try to make themselves appear to be that which best accomplishes that purpose.

However, it's the big things to which I do pay rapt attention. If you're trying to sell me a house or car, gain my business or friendship, tell me why I'm not getting a raise or otherwise significantly impact my life, then you have my full and undivided attention. At that point in time, I'm evaluating what I know about you, how you've acted in the past, and what you are saying and doing in that moment in time.

Can someone lie to me and get away with it? Certainly! Every day, in fact, I'm amused by some of the things people try to pull, and I still know that I'm missing a large percentage of the deception going on around me. I'm aware that my friends aren't always who they portray themselves to be and that the same goes for my enemies. And sometimes, I trust my enemies more so than my friends. Your enemies, after all, are usually somewhat predicable (and you already know to take whatever they say with a proverbial grain of salt). I even, upon occasion, have clients who hire me to help them to assist in clearing their names of wrongdoing, yet somehow believe I won't catch their deception and realize they are guilty after all. I recently had a client—a judge, of all things!—demand I return his retainer fee after I provided a report stating I believed he was deceptive in his sexual harassment interview. He apparently thought he was buying me, not my services, when he signed my contract.

But I choose my battles much more wisely than I did than when I was in my twenties and even when I was in my thirties. Now, it has to truly matter before I call Pinocchio a liar or even care if she's lying. Pinocchio's deception must personally and adversely affect me or those I care about before I make a move. And even then, I now stop to consider why Pinocchio is lying before I act.

I realize there was a lot of information to absorb in this book. By the time you finish it, you'll want to rush out and start catching liars yourself.

But before you start looking for the truth, **make sure you want to find it.** Pinocchio wears many disguises, but he or she sometimes tells lies with only the best of intentions. Honesty is the most valuable currency we can possess in our society, but it is hard-won currency. Once you are assured you are being dealt with honestly in business, love, and life, you will find that your very existence will be less hectic and stressful.

References

Ames, A. (2007) Mind control for video games. {Online}. Available: http://www.pcworld.com/article/id,129670-c,techindustrytrends/article.html

Bandler, R. & Grinder, J. (1975) The structure of magic I. Palo Alto, CA: Science and Behavior Books.

Bandler, R. & Grinder, J. (1979). Frogs into princes. Maob, UT: Real People Press.

Biafra, J. (1986). Lie detector. On Bedtime for democracy (LP). USA: Alternative tentacles.

Buckner, M., Meara, N.M., Reese, E.J, & Reese, M. (1987). Eye movement as an indicator of sensory components in thought. Journal of Counseling Psychology, 3, 283-287.

Cialdini, R. (2006). Persuasion: The psychology of influence. USA: Collins.

Collidi, C. Le Avventure Di Pinocchio: Storia di Un Burrattino. (1986). (N.J. Perella, Trans.).London: University of California Press, Ltd. (Original work published 1883.)

DePaulo, B. (1986). On the job experience and detection of deception. Journal of Applied Social Psychology, 16, 249-267.

DePaulo, B. (1992). Nonverbal behavior and self presentation. Psychological Bulletin, 111, 203-243.

DePaulo, B. (1994). Spotting lies: Can humans learn to do better? Current Directions in Psychological Science, 3, 83-86.

DeForges, D. & Lee, T. (1995). Detecting deception is not as easy as it seems. Teaching of Psychology, 22, 128-130.

115

Dillingham, C. (1995).Traditional v. modern interview techniques. The Chief of Police, 2, 60-62.

Dillingham, C. (1998). Would Pinocchio's Eyes Have Revealed His Lies?. Unpublished master's thesis, University of Central Florida, Florida.

Dilts, R. (1983). Roots of Neuro-Linguistic Programming. Cupertino, CA: Meta Publications.

Ekman, P. (2004). Emotions revealed: recognizing faces and feelings to improve communication and emotional life. USA: First Owl Books.

Ekman, P. (1997). The truth behind the liar. SoundPrint. [Online]. Available: http://www.soundprint.org/~science/truth_behind_liar.html.

Ekman, P. (1985). Telling lies: clues to deceit in the marketplace, politics, and marriage. NY, New York: W.W. Norton & Company, Inc.

Ekman, P. & Friesen, W. (1969). Nonverbal leakage and clues to deception. Psychiatry, 32, 88-106.

Ekman, P. & Friesen, W. (2003). Unmasking the face: a guide to recognizing emotions from facial clues. Cambridge, MA: Malor Books.

Ekman, P. & Friesen, W. (1972). Hand movements. Journal of Communication, 22, 353-374.

Ekman, P., Friesen, W., & Scherer, K. (1976). Body movement and voice pitch in deceptive interaction. Semiota, 16, 23-27.

Ekman, P. & O'Sullivan, M. (1991). Who can catch a liar? American Psychologist, 46, 913-920.

Ekman, P., O'Sullivan, M., Friesen, W., & Scherer, K. (1991). Invited article: face, voice, and body in detecting deceit. Journal of Nonverbal behavior, 15, 125.

Federal Bureau of Investigation Law Enforcement Communication Division (1995, September). Neuro-Linguistic programming. Interviewing. 18-21.

Gilmore, D. & Samson, P. (1994). Keep talking. On *The division bell* (CD). USA: Columbia Records.

Goleman, D. (2007). Flame first, think later: New clues to e-mail misbehavior. {Online}. Available: http://www.nytimes.com/2007/02/20/health/psychology/20essa.html?ex=1173416400&en=1053195ef4a8f26d&ei=5070

Gray, R. (1991). Tools for the trade: Neuro-Linguistic programming and the art of communication. Federal Probation, 55, 11-16.

Grinder, J. & Bandler, R. (1976). The structure of magic II. Palo Alto, CA: Science and Behavior Books.

Harmon, R. & O'Neil, C. (1981). Neurolinguistic programming for counselors. Personnel and Guidance Journal, 59, 449-453.

Henley, D. & Frey, G. (1975). Lyin' Eyes. On *One of these nights* (LP). USA: Asylum.

Horvath, F., Jayne, B., & Buckley, J. (1994). Differentiation of truthful and deceptive criminal suspects. Journal of Forensic Science 3, 793-807.

Inbau, F., Reid, J. & Buckley, J. (1986). Criminal interrogations and confessions, third edition. Baltimore, MD: Williams & Wilkins.

Irsay, S. (2002). Fear factor: How far can police go to get a confession? {Online}. Available: http://news.findlaw.com/court_tv/s/20021119/19nov2002122233.html

Jagger, M. & Richards, K. (1968). You can't always get what you want. On *Let it bleed* (LP). UK: Decca Records/ABKCO.

Kraut, R. (1978). Verbal and nonverbal cues in the perception of lying. Journal of Personality and Social Psychology, 36, 380-391.

Leone, C. (1977). Accuracy in the Detection of Deception as a Function of Training in the Study of Human Behavior. Unpublished master's thesis, University of Central Florida, Florida.

Lesce, T. (1990). SCAN: Deception detection by scientific content analysis. {online}. Available: http://www.lsiscan.com/id37.htm

Lieberman, D.J. (1998). Never be lied to again. New York, NY: St. Martin's Press.

McLish, M. (2001). I know you are lying: detecting deception through statement analysis. Winterville, N.C.: PoliceEmployment.com.

McVie, C. & Quintela, E. (1987). Little lies. On Tango in the night (LP). USA: Reprise.

Reid & Associates (2003). Laughter and the Detection of Deception—Tip of the Month from John E. Reid & Associates. {Online}. Available: https://www.policeone.com/products/articles/69462/

Rhoads, S. & Solomon, R. (1987). Subconscious rapport building: Another approach to interviewing. The Police Chief, 4, 39-41.

Rollins, H. (1994). Liar (CD). USA: Imago.

Ryan., H. (2007). Nurse on trial for husband's murder can't testify about passing polygraph, judge says. {Online). Available: http://www.courttv.com/trials/mcguire/040507_ctv.html?link=eaf

Shore, D. (Writer) & Barclay, P. (Producer). House. Three stories (Episode 121). USA: Fox

Storace, M. & Von Arb, F. (1984). Our love (LP). On The Blitz. USA: Spitfire.

Uniform Crime Reports Section, Federal Bureau of Investigation. (1992, September). Killed in the line of duty: A study of selected felonious killings of law enforcement officers. Washington, DC. 9-23.

Vasques, M. (2005). Don't lie. On Monkey business (CD). USA: A&M/Interscope.

Vrij, A. (1993). Credibility judgements of detectives: The impact of nonverbal behavior, social skills, and physical characteristics on impression formation. Journal of Social Psychology, 133, 601-610.

Vrij, A. (1995). Behavioral correlates of deception in a simulated police interview. Journal of Psychology, 129, 15-28.

Vrij, A. (1996). Lie experts' beliefs about nonverbal indicators of deception. Journal of Nonverbal Behavior, 20 (1), 65-80.

Vrij, A. (1997). Nonverbal communication and credibility. In A. Memon, A. Vrij, & R. Bull. Accuracy and perceived credibility of suspects, victims, and witnesses. New York: McGraw-Hill.

Vrij, A. & Lochun, S. (1997). Neuro-Linguistic programming and the police: Worthwhile or not? Journal of Police and Criminal Psychology, 12 (1), 25-31.

Vrij, A. & Winkel, F. (1993). Objective and subjective indicators of fraud. Issues in Criminology and Legal Psychology, No. 20.

Walters, S. B. (1996). Principles of Kinesic Interview and Interrogation. Boca Raton, FL: CRC Press, Inc.

Walters, S.B. (2000). The truth behind the liar: how to spot a lie and protect yourself from deception. Naperville, Il: Sourcebooks, Inc.

Wiseman, R. (1997). The truth behind the liar. SoundPrint. [Online]. Available: http://www.soundprint.org/~science/truth_behind_the_liar.html

Woolfson, E. & Parsons, A. (1983). Games people play. On *The best of the Alan Parsons Project* (LP). USA: Arista.

978-0-595-48751-6
0-595-48751-3

2805202

Made in the USA